Up a Country Lane Cookbook

A Bur Oak Original

Up a
Country Lane
Cookbook

By Evelyn Birkby

Foreword by
Jane and Michael Stern

UNIVERSITY OF IOWA PRESS 🄿 IOWA CITY

University of Iowa Press, Iowa City 52242

Design by Karen Copp

Printed on acid-free paper

Library of Congress Cataloging-in-Publication Data
Birkby, Evelyn.
    Up a country lane cookbook / by Evelyn
Birkby; foreword by Jane and Michael Stern.
        p.   cm. — (A Bur oak original)
    Includes index.
    ISBN 0-87745-420-5
    1. Cookery, American—Midwestern
style.   2. Farm life—Iowa.
I. Title.   II. Series.
TX715.2.M53B57   1993
641.5977—dc20   93-20659
                                              CIP

97 96 95 94 93 C 5 4 3 2 1

FOR MY FAMILY
And all the friends who shared
our years at Cottonwood Farm

Contents

~~~~~~~~~~

Foreword BY JANE AND MICHAEL STERN

W̲e have eaten a lot of very fine meals as we have traveled around the country the last twenty years, but there isn't one we remember more fondly than the time Evelyn Birkby invited us for supper at her house in Sidney, Iowa. We came to Evelyn's place because we were writing a story about her and other area radio homemakers, about how women—and men—of the midlands have depended on these kindly voices of the airwaves to cheer them up in the doldrums of a muddy spring, to provide company on bleak winter afternoons, and to share their favorite recipes throughout the years. Like a vast regional party line, Evelyn's own radio show (starting in 1950), along with the "Up a Country Lane" column that she began writing for the *Shenandoah Evening Sentinel* even before she was on the air, provided her with a network of friends—readers and listeners—who could always count on her for handy tips, sound advice, and, most important of all, steady companionship.

Evelyn greeted us at the front door as her husband, Robert, came around from the backyard garden, nibbling on some just-picked wild plums that looked like cherry tomatoes. We ate at twilight on the screened sun porch in back of the house attached to the kitchen; we could look out at the garden, listen to a family of nesting wrens, and see the monitoring equipment Robert uses to report conditions to the United States Weather Service in Des Moines.

Evelyn prepared what she called a real Iowa dinner—a collection of some of her favorite things to cook and eat, every one of which had a story to go with it. As a woman who is a newspaper columnist and has been a professional radio host, she guided us through the meal with enthusiasm and a contagious sense of humor, taking every opportunity to enthrall us with the rural customs that have never ceased to enthrall her. Evelyn relishes the nuances of homemaking and recipe swapping, and her passion for the stitched homily samplers on her kitchen wall as well as the pork chops in her oven was impossible to resist.

The meal began with a preface about her trip to buy the pork in the nearby town of Farragut, where the butcher assured her that the evening's chops actually came from an Iowa pig. They were prepared according to a recipe Evelyn got from Virginia Miller, a long-time reader of her column, listener to her radio broadcasts, and friend who lives in an old farmhouse east of Anderson. Over the years Evelyn has shared many of Virginia's recipes with her other readers and listeners. This one is called Elegant Pork Chops, and it yielded a dish that was succulent and satisfying: hefty plateaus of pork marshaled in a baking pan bubbling with thick red syrup. They were as tender as pot roast, and the meat pulled from the bone with a gentle tug of the fork, venting wisps of sweet, piggy perfume.

With the pork chops, Evelyn served steamed corn on the cob from the Birkby garden, allotting four ears per person. On a big plate next to the bowl of corn were a tub of low-fat margarine and a stick of butter. (Everybody at the table that festive night chose the latter.) Also on the side were broiled tomato halves topped with seasoned bread crumbs, pickled beets, a salad topped with locally made country-style dressing that Evelyn lightened with a little beaten egg white, and a loaf of hard-crust seven-grain bread, for which Evelyn apologized: only five grains had been used. To garnish the bread, in addition to the margarine and butter, Evelyn provided honey from Robert's apiary, blackberry and currant jelly, and strawberry preserves (all from his fruit). The gooseberries in the gooseberry tart at dessert were Birkby fruit, too; but the lemon chiffon ice cream dished out as silky orbs atop each portion of tart had been store-bought in the town of Shenandoah, made from a recipe developed by the Falk sisters over in Essex.

Everything at that meal was connected to people Evelyn knew and to the Iowa she loves. It wasn't just food; it was stories, it was neighbors, it was a single supper that sang about a whole way of life. And that is what we adore about this cookbook Evelyn has written. It isn't only recipes. It is the biography of a community. It is fun and entertaining and useful; but perhaps more important than any of these good things, it is a true portrait of an era not so long ago and a place that doesn't seem so far away, and the people who lived there and the times and rituals they shared.

Farm life in the years after World War II as Evelyn Birkby describes it wasn't a pretty pastoral idyll. It was hard; she and Robert knew more than their share of tragedy. And this book freely tells about the struggles as well as the triumphs of the life they knew. How refreshing it is to read a rural cookbook that isn't only rosy imaginings of bountiful harvests, groaning boards, and joyful celebrations at every mealtime. There is plenty of happiness in Evelyn's story of life on the farm, but it is happiness, like the recipes, that flows out of the reality of everyday existence and means so much more because of the hard work from which it comes.

Similarly, the recipes in this book are not the kind of utopian ones that so many cookbook writers contrive when they want to invent a sanitized picture of farm life designed to appeal to trendy foodies who have recently been told by a gourmet magazine that midwestern food is chic. You won't find any recipes for goat cheese timbales (the Birkbys had no goats) or odd-shaped pasta al dente (Evelyn calls it spaghetti). These are recipes for dishes that neighbors really cook and eat: bread and butter pickles, pork chow mein with noodles from a can, chicken pie served with carrot biscuits, stockyard stew, gelatinized buttermilk salad, and hot milk cake.

Evelyn Birkby knows her subject; she has lived in Iowa nearly all her life. But the special enchantment of this book comes from the fact that farm housewifery never came naturally to her. Although she was raised in small town Iowa, her father was a minister, not a farmer, and Evelyn once told us that as a child she was always a dreamer. When she and Robert got married, they shared a dream: to have their own farm. They were enraptured with an ideal, so they took the plunge. Even when it didn't work out as they had planned, Evelyn never lost her affection for the lore and charms of country living—white laundry flapping on the line, sweet berry pies emerging from the oven, Thursday-morning steak and eggs from the weekly corn-fed beef club, and the soul-enriching pleasures of visiting with friends. Her fondness for the farm, the neighbors, and the honest humanity of rural life is what has made her newspaper columns so popular for more than forty years, and it is what makes *Up a Country Lane* such an uplifting book to read.

Evelyn writes that the way of life she recalls from her country lane has all but vanished now. The day of the close communities of small family farms has passed. But this book is so much more than sweet nostalgia for a bygone era. It is an enlightening piece of American history. We are grateful Evelyn has shared her memories and her zeal and the wisdom of the place where she has lived.

Acknowledgments

~~~~~~

My heartfelt thanks to all the neighbors, friends, and relatives who helped me relive the 1940s and 1950s in rural Iowa, to those who provided me with their wonderful photographs, and to photographer Mark Jewel of Sidney, Iowa, who made the pictures into usable prints.

I am grateful to the publishers of the *Shenandoah Evening Sentinel* for permission to use material from my "Up a Country Lane" columns and from their photo files and to all the loyal readers who through the years have shared their best recipes with me. I wish to express my gratitude to the enthusiastic staff at the University of Iowa Press who found the stories, photographs, and recipes of this era important and exciting enough to preserve.

A special thank-you to my family, Robert, Bob, Jeff, and Craig, who ate all the food I prepared as I tested recipes and who urged me to put them into a book and then make it more than just a cookbook. I am indebted to son Bob, who lived all those years with us on Cottonwood Farm, who helped me envision this book, and who assisted me every step along the way as it took shape.

Introduction

～～～～～～～～～～

The middle of the twentieth century is marked by the year 1950, but the division of events in this hundred-year span really came in 1946 at the end of the Second World War. The years following that war were a time of enormous change. Soldiers returned home to find old patterns shattered by the conflict and new technology developing that soon altered the way people lived and worked. Many of those returnees came to rural Mid-America, where farming was the predominant way of life.

The people who resided in southwest Iowa half a century ago built their lives around the land, their families, their neighborhoods, their schools, and their churches. They reflected the independent, hard-working pioneer spirit that had motivated their ancestors to come to this country. Life became easier after the war as crews installed electrical lines into houses and barns to run machines formerly powered by hand. Travel became simpler as roads were improved. The increasing number of telephone companies with their extended lines brought voices from other homes and cities to people wherever they lived.

As we look back from the present, farm life in the 1940s and 1950s often appears idyllic, but underneath the pastoral exterior were threats of storms, droughts, ruined crops, low prices, sickness, and accidents.

A family on a small farm could have more than its share of isolation, loneliness, and constant need for hard, physical labor. So the memories of simple, happy events and celebrations must realistically be tempered by the struggles endured.

My husband, Robert, had been born and raised in southwest Iowa, far more a rural product than I. Following service in the U.S. Army Air Corps, he returned home after the war and became a district Boy Scout executive, but he always carried the dream of having his own farm. That dream led us to Cottonwood Farm.

Although I was raised in small towns in Iowa, I came to marriage and, later, the farm fresh from three years living in the heart of Chicago. The perspective this change in life-style gave me was valuable as I learned to relate to the people who had always lived in a rural setting. The more I became acquainted with my neighbors and experienced a similar pattern of existence, the more I appreciated their ingenuity, intelligence, energy, fortitude, and friendliness.

From my vantage point in Mill Creek Valley I saw life in rural and small town Iowa with all of its fluxes and changes, its troubles and joys. Since 1949, I have written a weekly column for the *Evening Sentinel*, a Shenandoah, Iowa, daily newspaper. My "Up a Country Lane" column has given me a forum in which to share my observations about my own experiences and those of my neighbors.

As a newcomer I quickly learned that my farm neighbors fed far more than their own families. Their chickens went into the soup factories in Chicago and Kansas City. Area creameries made locally produced cream into butter and shipped great quantities to Hershey, Pennsylvania, to be made into chocolates. Iowa grains became loaves of bread or boxes of oatmeal or were fed to livestock which found their way as steaks and chops and roasts onto tables from coast to coast.

Without question, produce was the lifeblood of the farm community into which we moved, but it was more than a source of income and sustenance for bodies. Rural families used food at church suppers and community picnics to create settings where friendships flourished. Meals cemented family bonds as parents and children sat around the kitchen table together to eat and share experiences.

Between the covers of this book are stories and photographs of a way of life which is all but gone. It is a glimpse of rural midwestern life as it was lived during the decade immediately following World War II. Included are recipes treasured by readers of my "Up a Country Lane" columns.

These are my favorite recipes as well. I often adjust some of the ingredients to meet today's dietary standards. I use low-calorie margarine instead of lard or butter, more egg whites than egg yolks, 2% or skimmed milk instead of whole milk, half-and-half or prepared whipped topping instead of cream. I check current canning recommendations to be certain I process foods the proper length of time. Smaller amounts of salt and sugar are healthier but do not make the food any less tasty.

But once in a while, just for the fun of it, I make up a pie crust with lard, ice cream with many eggs, or bread pudding laced with cream. I prepare recipes with the ingredients I can find that most nearly resemble those we had close at hand in the days my family and I lived up that country lane. Then I revel in the taste of foods as they were first created by women who cultivated their own garden produce, who had milk and cream fresh from their cows, and who had farm-raised meats with which to cook.

Now you can reprise the dishes from those simple meals, those frequent potlucks, those delightful club luncheons, those bountiful harvest feasts, and those sparkling holiday gatherings. As you lay out the platters, bowls, and pie plates filled with these treasures, I hope you will also build memories with your own family and friends.

Up a Country Lane Cookbook

1. Mill Creek Valley

~~~~~~~~~~~~~~~~~~~~~~~~~~~~~~~~~~~~~~~

Two miles south of the town of Farragut in southwest Iowa the road changes from pavement to gravel and asphalt reminiscent of an earlier time before the network of paved rural roads and great interstate highways stretched across the state. Follow the road another four miles and you'll come to the top of a hill where, if you pause long enough, you can fill your eyes and your soul with the sight of a pleasant, lush valley. It lies low in undulating hills like a small gem in a sunshine-filled jewel box.

In the center of this gentle valley, Mill Creek weaves its erratic way across the landscape. The sun glints on the water, and several giant cottonwoods stand like sentinels along the bank. A few Osage orange hedges lift their rugged, close-growing branches near the creek and in a field or two, reminding you that pioneer farmers passed this way. In an arching clear blue sky, a hawk lifts on thermal winds and glides silently over the green fields.

The shape of the valley and the wanderings of the creek are the same today as they were in 1948 when my husband, Robert, and I first looked down from this hill, but so much else has changed. Today, a few farmers with enormous machines can cultivate and harvest the crops of the entire valley. Gone are many of the farmsteads that were

1

The lane at Cottonwood Farm. My son, Bob, and I wait with our dog, Sparkle, for daughter Dulcie Jean to arrive home on the school bus. Robert Birkby is on the tractor next to the barn at the rear of the photo.

once scattered along the road. Gone are most of the people who once lived here, worked the land, and raised their families. Gone, most of all, is the special way of living that was midwestern farm life of the 1940s and 1950s.

But what we saw almost fifty years ago was our dream at the end of a long, curved dirt lane. There was a barn, hog shed, corn crib, equipment shed, and chicken house. A narrow path led from the barnyard to a woodshed and then to a small, white, single-story house like so many others across the countryside.

The 120 acres of rich black farmland surrounding the house presented us with the opportunity to discover whether we could make it as farmers. Many other veterans like Robert were returning from World War II eager to rent farms and put down roots in a place they could

Our house at Cottonwood Farm had five rooms and a large screened-in back porch.

call their own. While farming was new to us—Robert had grown up in a small town nearby, and I had most recently lived and worked in downtown Chicago—we shared with many other young married couples the eagerness to build meaningful lives on the farm for ourselves and our children.

We called our new home Cottonwood Farm. As we moved in, I discovered that the gentle rise of the hills hid most of the other farmyards from my view, creating a place very different from the rush of the city I had known. I did treasure the quiet peacefulness of the countryside and appreciated it even more as I came to realize the close-knit qualities of those families beyond my view. I fervently hoped my own family would be woven into the fabric of this neighborhood. Even though I could not see them, I was always conscious of the fact that just over the rise in the land stood other farms with other households. Many of these families had been in the area for a very long time.

Europeans began settling this land before 1850, coming up the Missouri River and then along the Nishnabotna River into which Mill Creek flows. Many had emigrated from other countries to escape harsh laws, overpopulation, unrest, conscription, poverty, and war. They were attracted to the Midwest by the productive soil and the beauty of the countryside.

The names I saw on the mailboxes up and down our road reflected the heritage of the farm families. The ancestors of the Schnoors, Brickers, Nelsons, and Brookses had come from Germany. The Phairs (who changed their name on the journey to the phonetic spelling, Fair) came from Scotland and the Finleys from Ireland. The Troxels and a Tzand arrived from Switzerland. A few early settlers had not wanted the country of their origin or the reason for their coming disclosed. They changed their names and talked only vaguely about the Old Country, leaving hurts and identities behind.

Some of the pioneer farmers arrived with enough money to purchase land. Others worked as hired hands to get a start. The single women often worked as domestics in farm homes, where a number of them met the men they eventually married. The women bore the children, cared for the homes, and helped their husbands. They became instrumental in founding churches and schools. They blended a remarkable mixture of cultural, national, and religious backgrounds into the families living around Mill Creek Valley.

The descendants of those early pioneers were our nearest neighbors. When Robert and I arrived with our two children to try to fit into this settled farm community, we discovered that several families, like Millard (known as Bill) and Ferrell Allely and their three children, were newcomers like us, renting land with the same hope of someday owning their own farms. The lives of renters were less settled, less comfortable, and far less secure than those of farm families who owned their land. We could have been viewed as outsiders, but the long-time residents by and large accepted us as friends and co-workers. Part of this warmth and understanding could have been the result of the memories many of our neighbors had of their own struggles or those of their relatives.

Portraits I saw in some of the farmhouses introduced me to the first settlers of this neighborhood. There was, for example, the faded likeness of James Utterback, who came up the Missouri River to southwest Iowa in about 1838. There was the Simmerman family, who had ar-

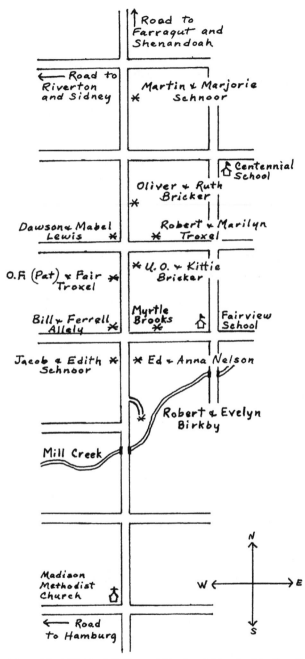

Map of the Mill Creek Valley neighborhood. Map by Marilyn Troxel.

My sister, Ruth Bricker (left), and my mother, Mae Corrie (right), sit at the top of the steps of Oliver and Ruth's "big house." Although it was not larger than many of the other houses in the neighborhood, it was larger than the nearby homeplace where Oliver's parents lived.

rived in the eastern United States from England before the Revolutionary War. When that conflict began, the family found the anti-English sentiment threatening and moved west by covered wagon to escape prejudice. Eventually, descendants of those first Simmermans arrived in southwest Iowa. The Utterback and Simmerman lines merged to produce, eventually, Mabel Simmerman Lewis, who owned property near our Cottonwood Farm. There was Walter Brooks, who purchased his farm in 1874 from speculators who had bought many acres of prairie and then resold the land to newcomers as they arrived. And there was Ed Nelson, whose father, Nels, had purchased the place just north of Cottonwood Farm in 1915. In 1921, Ed and his wife, Anna, brought their possessions up from Missouri and moved to the modest farmhouse and gradually added seven children to their family. Ed later inherited the land when Nels died.

Up the road a piece, pictures of my own paternal Scottish Corrie ancestors hung on the living room wall of my sister Ruth's home. Ruth

O. F. (Pat) and Fair Troxel near their home. Bob Troxel photo.

had married Oliver Bricker in 1941 and moved to the "big house" on his farm, part of extensive holdings of his Swedish and German pioneer grandparents and his father's. It was from Oliver that we rented Cottonwood Farm.

Ownership of the land passed from one generation to the next, marriages often blending neighboring families and farms. Fair Finley's family had emigrated from Ireland (her first name was from her mother's surname). After the death of her mother, Fair stayed in the home to do the housework for her father. She married O. F. (Pat) Troxel, a local man who, when they married, moved into the Finley household. When Fair's father died, the land passed to Fair and then to her son, Bob.

Along with the Nelsons, Jacob and Edith Schnoor were our neighbors immediately north of Cottonwood Farm. Jacob had left Germany in 1898 to escape conscription. He came through Ellis Island carrying all of his possessions in one small trunk. While working in the Chicago stockyards he met Martin Dresher, an Iowa farmer of German extraction, who had come into the city with a load of cattle. Delighted to find someone with whom he could converse, Jacob returned to southwest Iowa with Mr. Dresher to work as his hired man. Despite meager wages of fifteen dollars per month plus room and board, Jacob saved enough over the next nineteen years and became so much a part of the Dresher family that, when Mr. Dresher retired, Jacob rented the land and, a few years later, bought the farm.

Edith Ackley was one of five sisters of Dutch background. She came to work as a housekeeper at the Dresher farm, where romance blossomed. She and Jacob were married in 1910. Twenty-four years younger than Jake, Edith assisted in running the farm and in raising their four children.

The eighteen-room house where Jacob and Edith Schnoor lived was larger than the others in the neighborhood, reflecting the wealth and the interests of the owners. Behind the house stood a tremendous barn that was reminiscent of both the Dreshers' and Schnoors' German heritage. Jake called his place Osage Farms, named for the tough, gnarled Osage orange hedges pioneer farmers planted as fences around livestock pastures.

For those who owned farms and for those of us who were renting, the land was of central importance. From it came the crops that made rural life possible. The history of every acre was closely aligned with the histories of local families, tying them together with the richness of the soil as well as by blood and by common concerns.

And, like the soil, the varied heritages of our neighbors gave the area a culture and a cuisine all its own. Farm women prepared the Old Country recipes their mothers and grandmothers had taught them. Shared at church potlucks, social gatherings, and neighborhood holiday dinners, those recipes evolved over the years, flowing and changing through the generations to become a distinctly midwestern way of preparing food. In rural Middle America, the melting pot had become a cooking kettle.

Fair Troxel's Frosted Ginger Creams

1 cup sugar
1 cup sorghum or molasses
1/2 cup butter, softened
1/2 cup margarine, softened
3 egg yolks
3 teaspoons baking soda

2/3 cup hot water
1 teaspoon ginger
1 teaspoon cinnamon
1/2 teaspoon salt
5 1/2 to 6 cups flour

Combine first four ingredients and cream well. Beat egg yolks with a fork or whisk and beat into first mixture. Dissolve baking soda in hot water and blend in. Combine seasonings and 5 cups of flour. Add and beat well. Stir in enough additional flour to make a soft dough which will hold its shape when dropped from a teaspoon on a greased cookie sheet. Or chill dough and then roll out about 1/4 to 1/2 inch thick and make into cutout cookies. Bake at 375 degrees for 5 to 8 minutes or until lightly browned. Makes about 6 dozen.

WHITE FLUFFY FROSTING

3 egg whites
2 1/4 cups sugar

1/4 cup water
1 teaspoon flavoring

Beat egg whites until soft peaks form. Boil sugar and water together until it spins a thread, about 275 degrees on a candy thermometer. Pour hot syrup over egg whites, beating constantly until frosting is thick. Add flavoring and continue beating until it begins to get firm. Spread on baked cookies and sprinkle with coconut.

Fair always made these cookies with lard. She made large cookies and frosted them with a generous amount of frosting. Fair always put a raisin in the center of her cookies; it was her trademark.

Edith Schnoor's Spice Cake

1 1/2 cups sugar
1/2 cup butter or margarine
3 eggs
1/2 cup sour milk
3 cups flour
4 teaspoons cocoa
1 teaspoon cloves

1 teaspoon cinnamon
1 teaspoon nutmeg
1 cup raisins
1 cup black walnuts (or other nuts)
1/2 teaspoon baking soda
1 tablespoon hot water

Cream together the sugar and butter or margarine. Beat in the eggs and sour milk. (You can make your own sour milk by adding 1 teaspoon of vinegar to 1 cup of sweet milk. Let stand 5 minutes to sour.) Sift flour with cocoa and spices and stir into batter. Add raisins and nuts. Dissolve baking soda in hot water and add last. Bake in a greased and floured 9-by-13-inch cake pan at 350 degrees for 35 to 40 minutes. Makes about 15 pieces.

Ruth Bricker's Banana Bread

1/2 cup butter or margarine
1 cup sugar
2 egg yolks
1 cup mashed ripe bananas
1/2 cup cold water
2 cups flour

1 teaspoon baking powder
1 teaspoon baking soda
1/2 teaspoon salt
1/2 cup nuts
2 egg whites

Cream butter or margarine and sugar. Beat in egg yolks. Blend in bananas and cold water. Combine dry ingredients and mix into batter. Add nuts. Beat egg whites until stiff peaks form and fold in. Spoon into greased and floured bread pan and bake at 375 degrees for 1 hour. Let stand several hours or overnight. Ruth likes to make several loaves, let them cool, wrap them in foil, and freeze them for unexpected company or for later meals. Makes 1 loaf.

Food for the Gods

2 teaspoons baking powder
1 cup sugar
3 large or 4 small eggs, well
    beaten

9 tablespoons coarse soda cracker
    crumbs
1/2 pound English walnuts
1/2 pound dates, coarsely chopped

Combine baking powder and sugar, add eggs, and beat well. Stir in remaining ingredients. Add a little cream or half-and-half if needed to make mixture stick together. Pat into a greased 9-by-12-inch pan. Bake 30 minutes at 350 degrees. Cut into squares or rectangles and serve with whipped cream or whipped topping. Marilyn Troxel acquired this recipe from her mother, Hazel Myers. No one remembers why it was given this name, except for the wonderful flavor and mixture of ingredients—no doubt it is food the gods would enjoy. Makes 15 to 21 bars.

English Oatmeal Spice Cookies

1 cup raisins
5 tablespoons juice from raisins
1 cup sugar
1 cup shortening
2 eggs, beaten
2 cups rolled oats, toasted
1 to 2 tablespoons butter or
    margarine

1/4 teaspoon salt
1 teaspoon baking soda
1/2 teaspoon cinnamon
1/2 teaspoon allspice
1/2 teaspoon nutmeg
2 cups flour
1 teaspoon vanilla flavoring
1/2 cup chopped nuts

Cover raisins with water and simmer 3 minutes. Drain, reserving liquid. Cream sugar and shortening together. Beat in the eggs. Stir in raisins and 5 tablespoons raisin liquid. Toast rolled oats—either old-fashioned or quick—in 1 to 2 tablespoons of butter or margarine in a skillet, stirring. Cool and combine with remaining dry ingredients and mix into first mixture. Add flavoring and nuts. Drop from a teaspoon on greased cookie sheet and bake at 350 degrees about 8 minutes or until brown on top. Makes about 4 dozen.

Neighbor's Low-Calorie Lasagna

1 pound ground beef
1 clove garlic, minced
1 tablespoon sweet basil flakes or
   leaves
1/2 teaspoon salt
2 cups canned tomatoes
1 6-ounce can tomato paste
1 8-ounce can tomato sauce

12 to 14 lasagna noodles
3 cups ricotta cheese or creamy
   cottage cheese
1/4 cup grated Romana cheese
1/4 cup grated Parmesan cheese
2 tablespoons parsley flakes
2 eggs, slightly beaten
thinly sliced mozzarella cheese

Brown meat and drain. Add garlic, basil, salt, tomatoes, and tomato paste and sauce. Simmer uncovered for 30 minutes, stirring occasionally. Cook lasagna noodles in large amount of salted water for 8 to 10 minutes. Cool. Rinse in cool water so they can be handled. Grease 9-by-13-inch pan; place layer of noodles in pan. Combine ricotta or cottage cheese with Romana and Parmesan cheeses (grated fresh), parsley, and eggs. Spoon half this cheese mixture on the noodles, then a layer of mozzarella cheese, lapped a bit to make a solid layer, then one-third of the meat mixture. Repeat layers. End with a third noodle layer plus a thin layer of meat mixture on top. Sprinkle grated Romana cheese over top. This can be made several hours ahead of time and kept in the refrigerator until time to bake. Bake at 375 degrees for 30 minutes uncovered or up to 1 hour if covered or if ingredients are cold from storing in the refrigerator. Let stand 10 minutes before cutting into squares so filling will set and layers will not slide. This recipe reached the neighborhood via a Farragut teacher of Italian background who lived with his family for a time in the U. O. Bricker house. Makes 12 servings.

Pumpkin Pie

2 unbaked single-crust pie shells
2 cups brown sugar, packed
2 teaspoons cinnamon
1 teaspoon ginger
1 teaspoon allspice
1/2 teaspoon salt

2 tablespoons flour
2 3/4 cups canned pumpkin
4 eggs, slightly beaten
1 cup whipping cream
2 cups milk
2 teaspoons vanilla flavoring

Prepare 2 single-crust pie shells. Combine dry ingredients in a large bowl. Add the pumpkin. Mix the remaining ingredients and add to first mixture. Pour into two unbaked pie shells and bake at 400 degrees for 55 minutes or until a knife blade inserted into the filling comes out clean. The first time Marilyn Troxel made pumpkin pies from this, her mother Hazel Myers's recipe, she put them on the back step to cool and the dog ate them. It was a hard lesson for a new bride. Makes 2 pies.

Marilyn's Cranberry Ice

12 ounces fresh cranberries
2 1/2 cups water

1 1/2 cups sugar
2 1/4 tablespoons fresh lemon juice

Cook cranberries in water until they stop popping. Run through food mill or a sieve to remove the skins. Add sugar and lemon juice and mix well. Line muffin tins with paper or foil baking cups, fill with mixture, and freeze. The frozen sherbet can be served by removing paper and placing in sherbet glasses. You can double the recipe and store extras in a plastic bag in the freezer. Excellent for a dessert or a meat accompaniment or to clear the palate in the middle of a meal. Makes about 13 servings.

2. Gardening

~~~~~~~~~~~~~~~~~~~~~~~~~~~~~~~~~

The garden grown by a farm family was not a modest hobby enjoyed during leisure hours. Rather, it was a vital part of farm production, saving the family money on their food budget and sustaining them through times when income from crops and livestock was low. It also allowed the family to enjoy fresh fruits and vegetables brought to the table in prime condition. Juicy red tomatoes, crisp cucumbers and onions, sweet peas, ear corn, and green beans could be served just minutes after they had been picked. The flavor was incomparable.

Farm gardens were usually tucked behind the houses, though they could be anywhere, even in the front yard near the road where passersby could see the results of the growing year and judge the expertise of the gardener. Gardens visible from the road were often bordered with zinnias, marigolds, and bearded purple iris to brighten the area and help mask the sight of any weeds or crooked rows.

The farm wife was usually the family's gardener. While the ground was covered with snow, she would pore over the colorful catalogs mailed out each year by the seed and nursery companies and decide what her garden would contain. She might order by mail, assured by the companies that seeds would arrive just when they should be planted. Or she could go to the retail nursery stores in town in the spring to buy bean seeds, onion sets, strawberry plants, young berry bushes, and whatever else she needed.

Weather played a major role in the timing of garden planting. The earth had to be dry enough to crumble since plowing wet ground left hard clods rather than the fine soil best suited for the tender roots of sprouting seeds. The farmer took time out from plowing the fields to plow and harrow the garden. The teeth of the harrow broke up the clods and smoothed the soil. If the garden was too small for the heavy farm machinery, the farmer might use a spading fork to turn the dark earth by hand. With this part of the gardening done, the farmer would return to the fields.

The farm wife sowed the seeds, weeded the rows, sprayed the plants to kill bugs, and in dry spells watered the garden. As the produce ripened, she picked it, served some of it fresh to her family, then canned or froze the rest and stored it for use in the winter months when the garden no longer flourished.

Since I had not grown up in the country like so many of my neighbors, I moved to the farm with no gardening experience, but I was willing to give it a try. As our first spring in the country rolled around and the days became warm, Robert plowed a piece of ground near the house for our garden. He bought the seeds, handed me a hoe, gave me an encouraging smile, and returned to his field work.

I stood for a long time looking at the ground, fingering the seed packets and contemplating the hoe. I thought of the large gardens Fair Troxel and Anna Nelson and all the other farm women in the neighborhood were preparing near their homesteads. Surely I could master the techniques as well as they.

The directions on the packets of lettuce and pea and spinach seeds seemed simple enough—"Sow in straight rows one inch deep." Taking a deep breath, I pushed the hoe into the ground and pulled it along to make what I thought was a straight furrow. When I looked back though, the line of freshly turned earth was as crooked as the wiggly earthworms crawling in the soft dirt. Undeterred, I measured six inches over and started the next row. By the time I had dug four rows, the garden was beginning to resemble railroad switching tracks.

I persisted, making more rows, sowing the seeds, and covering them according to the directions. When nothing grew where or how I expected it to, Robert put the rest of the seeds in the ground and told me he would care for the plants with what time he could spare from his other work. I felt woefully inadequate.

"Our neighbors must have been born with hoes in their hands," I told Robert one evening as I peeled potatoes for supper. "Working in the garden never appealed to me, and my parents didn't teach me how. I'll learn how to cook and can the food, but I'm resigning as a gardener." I imagined that the garden gave a sigh of relief, for now it would have Robert's experienced hand to help it grow.

And grow it did. As fruits and vegetables appeared on branch and vine, I discovered the pleasure of picking them and preparing them for the table. I learned, for example, how to pick sweet corn, how to pull off the shucks as I walked to the house, and how to plunge the ears quickly into a pot of water already boiling on the stove. Fifteen minutes at most from garden to plate gave my family corn so sweet and tender it almost melted in our mouths.

I learned how to process garden produce for winter storage. When the work was done and I looked at the row of jars filled with ruby raspberry jelly, bright red strawberry jam, and golden marmalade, I felt a sense of real accomplishment. When my family spread the preserves I had made on slices of fresh, hot, homemade bread, their pleasure was a fitting reward for my labors.

With hundreds of small cucumbers hanging from the vines, I tried every pickle recipe my neighbors passed along to me—crystal pickles, dill pickles, bread and butter pickles, and chopped mixed pickles. I made seven-day, nine-day, and fourteen-day pickles; their names indicated how long the cucumbers had to soak in the brine and syrup to become pickles. Making pickles wasn't difficult, but it did involve many steps as I drained brine, heated syrup, put the mixture down in crocks, and marked the calendar for what day and what recipe I needed to attend to with which mixture. Eventually, I put the cucumbers-now-pickles into jars and sealed them tight.

When the pickles were done, I began canning green beans. I picked

Bob Birkby helps his Grandmother Corrie pick greens for a dinner salad. Women in the 1940s and 1950s generally wore dresses, and Grandma was no exception. Her polka-dot dress, sweater, nylon hose, and sensible shoes were normal attire for her to wear in the garden.

the beans and snapped them into inch-long pieces. While they pre-cooked in big pans on the gas range, I scalded quart-sized mason jars, then filled the jars with the beans and the boiling water in which they had cooked, added salt, and tightly screwed on the lids. The jars went into our National pressure canner on the stove. With the lid sealed, that canner pressure-processed the beans for thirty-five minutes, killing any microbes and creating a vacuum seal in the jars. Once the beans had cooled, I stored the jars in the cave behind the house.

Rural families felt fortunate to have a cave or root cellar for year-round storage of fruits, vegetables, and canned produce and as a safe refuge in case of tornadoes. Wooden steps led down to the hard earthen floor of our cave. Bricks lined the walls and low-domed roof. Several feet of dirt and sod covering the cellar kept the inside temperature cool

A National Pressure Canner was my primary kitchen helper during canning season. The brightly patterned wallpaper with its rural scene was typical of wall coverings in the 1940s and 1950s.

Craig Birkby delights in the generous crop of pumpkins he helped his father raise.

in the summer and above freezing in winter. A clay tile pipe embedded in the center of the ceiling allowed fresh air from the outside to circulate down inside the windowless space.

My spirits always rose as I carried jars of food down into the cave and lined them up on the wooden shelves along the wall. Each year as summer blended into fall, those shelves seemed to groan under their load of jars standing in neat, colorful rows—green beans and pickles, red beets, tomatoes, jellies, and juices. Wooden boxes and woven bushel baskets on the hard-packed dirt floor overflowed with potatoes and yams, butternut and acorn squash, pumpkins, carrots, and onions. The inside of that cave had a wonderful odor—a mixture of the aroma of dark earth combined with that of vegetables and fruits.

Autumn always brought treasures from the orchard: crisp red apples, rosy-skinned peaches, and golden pears ready to make into cobblers, salads, preserves, and apple butter, that refreshing, spicy brown spread which tastes good with almost anything that can use a sweet spread but is especially delicious combined with peanut butter.

By the middle of October, when we had completed the last picking of the tomatoes and beans, pulled up the remaining carrots, and plucked the last apple from the tree, Robert plowed the garden so it could lie fallow during the winter. The soil was ready to rest, and so was I.

End-of-the-Garden Relish

6 cups chopped green tomatoes
6 cups chopped red tomatoes
1 medium head cabbage
3 sweet red peppers
3 sweet green peppers
1 quart chopped onions
1 1/3 bunches celery

1/2 cup pickling salt
1 1/2 quarts cider vinegar
4 1/2 cups brown sugar, packed
4 1/2 inches stick cinnamon
1 1/2 teaspoons whole cloves
1 1/2 teaspoons mustard seeds

Chop or grind vegetables. Place in a large enamel or crockery container and sprinkle with salt. (Don't let the amount of salt deter you from making this relish; it is only to soften and prepare the vegetables to absorb the syrup. Most will be drained away.) Let mixture stand overnight. In the morning, drain well and put vegetables in a kettle, preferably enamel to keep from darkening. Add vinegar and brown sugar. Heat and stir to dissolve sugar. Tie spices in a bag or secure in a tea ball and add. Simmer (a slow bubble) for 30 minutes. Discard spices. Ladle chopped pickle mixture into sterilized jars, seal, and process according to current canning directions. This is a great recipe that uses up the last of the vegetables at the end of the growing season. Makes about 10 pints.

Bread and Butter Pickles

4 quarts medium-sized cucumbers,
  sliced
6 to 12 large onions, sliced
2 sweet green or red peppers, diced
  (optional)
1/2 cup pickling salt
3 cups cider vinegar

5 cups white or packed brown
  sugar
2 tablespoons turmeric
2 tablespoons mustard seeds
1 1/2 teaspoons celery seeds
1 1/2 teaspoons cinnamon

Simmer cucumbers, onions, and peppers in boiling water for 2 minutes to blanch. Drain. Place in bowl and pour 1/2 cup of pickling salt over them. Refrigerate for 12 hours with a weighted lid to keep from floating. (A pint jar filled with water and sealed with a tight lid makes a good weight.) Drain, rinse in cold water, and drain again thoroughly. Heat vinegar, sugar, and spices together, stir to dissolve sugar. When mixture starts to boil, add vegetables gradually. Stir as little as possible. Turn off fire and ladle pickles and syrup into hot sterilized jars and put on two-part lids. Process in boiling water bath for 15 minutes. Makes 8 pints.

Pickled Beets

3 quarts prepared beets
2 cups sugar
2 cups vinegar
2 cups water

1 teaspoon whole cloves
1 teaspoon whole allspice
1 stick cinnamon

Trim tops and stems down to 1 inch of top of beets. Do not cut into the beet itself or the color will bleed when the vegetable is cooked. Wash beets well. Cover with water and boil until beets are tender. Drain and cover with cold water. Slip off skins and trim off tops and roots. Slice if the beets are large. Combine sugar, vinegar, and 2 cups water to make syrup. Tie spices in a bag or a tea ball, combine with syrup, and bring to a boil. Add beets. Boil 10 minutes. Discard spices. Ladle into sterilized jars and seal. Ground spices can be used, but they tend to darken the beets. Either white or cider vinegar can be used. Makes 8 to 10 pints.

Lime Pickles

2 cups pickling lime
2 gallons water
1 to 1 1/2 gallons sliced cucumbers
8 cups cider vinegar

9 cups sugar
2 teaspoons salt
1 teaspoon mixed pickling spices
green food coloring

Dissolve the pickling lime in the water in a large crock, glass, plastic, or enamel container—not metal. Add fresh-from-the-garden washed and thickly sliced cucumbers—up to 1/2 inch thick. Weight down with a plate on top. (A pint jar filled with water with a tight screw lid placed on the plate will add weight to keep cucumbers from floating.) Toss a tea towel over the top to keep dust out. After 24 hours, drain and discard the lime water. Wash the cucumber slices through three waters (this gets rid of any lime residue, so don't worry about it remaining in the pickles). Return cucumbers to container and cover with cold water. Let stand 3 hours—*no longer*. Drain. In a large enamel kettle, make a syrup of vinegar, sugar, salt, and spices tied in a bag or secured in a tea ball. Bring mixture to a boil and add drained cucumbers. Turn off the fire. Cover and let stand overnight. In the morning, turn on the fire under kettle containing syrup, cucumbers, and spices. Bring to a boil and simmer on medium heat for 35 minutes. Add a few drops of green food coloring if desired to give a brighter color. Ladle into hot sterilized jars and seal. (Can be processed in boiling water for 10 minutes if desired.) A clove of garlic and a sprig of fresh dill added to each jar make a wonderful variation for this delightful sweet pickle. Makes 10 to 12 pints.

Watermelon Pickles

3 1/2 quarts prepared watermelon
   rind
water to cover
8 teaspoons alum

1 quart white vinegar
8 cups sugar
1 tablespoon whole cloves
2 sticks cinnamon

Trim off the green skin and pink flesh of the watermelon rind and discard. Cut remaining white part into cubes. When you have 3 1/2 quarts prepared, put in a large kettle, cover with water, and cook until just tender—about 20 minutes. Add alum to the water and let stand overnight. Drain. Rinse thoroughly, drain, and rinse a second time. Add to the rind the vinegar, sugar, and spices tied in a small cheesecloth bag or spooned into a large tea ball. Bring the mixture to a boil, stirring until sugar dissolves. Remove from the heat and let stand overnight. Again bring to a boil and remove from the heat. This time, let the watermelon pickles stand for 5 days. At the end of the 5 days, remove the spices and place cold pickles in sterilized jars. Place a few drops of food coloring in each jar if desired. (It is nice to add a little yellow to some, red to others, and green to a few to give variety and holiday sparkle. The color is absorbed completely through the pickles.) Cover with the cold syrup and seal. These are canned cold, no need to reheat. Makes about 7 pints.

Spiced Tomato Juice

1 cup finely chopped onion
1 cup chopped celery
8 quarts prepared tomatoes
4 to 6 sweet green peppers, chopped
1 tablespoon salt

1/4 cup sugar
2 to 3 bay leaves
1 tablespoon parsley flakes
1/2 teaspoon celery salt
1/2 teaspoon onion salt

Start onion and celery cooking with a little water as you prepare the tomatoes. Wash and quarter the tomatoes, take out any stems and white places. Do not peel. Add tomatoes to onions and celery, stir in the remaining ingredients, and bring the mixture to a boil. Simmer 15 minutes. Remove bay leaves and discard. Put tomato mixture through a food mill or colander to remove skins and seeds. Return to kettle and bring to rolling boil. Seal in hot sterilized jars. Process 15 minutes at 11 pounds pressure or in hot water bath, 35 minutes for pints and 40 minutes for quarts. Makes 8 to 10 quarts.

Strawberry Jam

6 cups strawberries
6 cups sugar

Wash strawberries, remove stems, and measure 2 cups of the berries and 2 cups sugar into a heavy 4- or 6-quart pan. Mash and simmer for 8 minutes, stirring occasionally. Add 2 more cups of whole berries and 2 more cups of sugar and continue cooking, stirring occasionally, for 8 minutes. Then add 2 cups of whole plump berries and 2 cups sugar, stir gently. Continue cooking for 8 more minutes. Ladle into hot sterilized jars and seal. Do not double the recipe, although several batches can simmer on the stove at the same time. Do not try to add more to a kettle than the directions given. If spring rains have been particularly abundant and the water content in the berries is more than normal, cook the jam 2 minutes more per boiling time to keep it from being too liquid. Robert's mother, Lucretia Birkby, introduced me to this excellent way to prepare strawberry jam. Makes about 7 cups.

Simple Grape Juice

Into each clean quart jar place 1 generous cup whole washed and stemmed Concord grapes and 1/3 cup sugar. Fill with boiling water to within 1 inch of the top. Screw on two-part canning lid. Continue until you have 7 quarts to fill the canner. Process in hot water bath for 15 minutes or in pressure canner at 5 pounds pressure for 10 minutes.

This makes a wonderful, clear, fresh-tasting grape juice to drink. It is not concentrated, so it need not be diluted. Make as much as you want.

Grape Jam

3 cups Concord grapes
3 cups sugar

Wash the grapes and remove the stems. Measure out 3 rounded cups and place in a heavy saucepan. Crush or mash slightly and add the sugar. Bring to a good rolling boil and continue boiling, stirring often, for 20 minutes. Remove from the fire and put the entire mixture through a food mill. Discard skins and seeds. Pour jam into sterilized jars or jelly glasses and top with melted paraffin. (Melt paraffin in a tin can which has been placed in a pan of water. Never melt directly over heat as it catches fire easily.) This jam can also be refrigerated or frozen for storage. Do not double the recipe, it is best when made in smaller portions. Makes 4 cups.

Fruit Marmalade

4 lemons
2 to 3 oranges
2 grapefruit

4 cups water
sugar

Peel the colored skin from the fruits and cut the peelings into fine strips or chop coarsely and put into a saucepan. Add water and simmer, stirring occasionally, until tender and somewhat transparent. Drain off water. Squeeze juice and pulp from fruits. Remove any seeds. Add juice and pulp to drained peel mixture. Simmer another 30 minutes. Add sugar desired—as much as an amount equal to the fruit mixture or a little less, according to your taste. Continue stirring and simmering until mixture thickens. It thickens more as it cools, so a little in a saucer cooled in the refrigerator will help you decide when the desired thickness is reached. Remove from fire, ladle into sterilized jars, seal, and process if desired. Can be refrigerated or frozen if preferred. Makes 4 to 5 half-pints.

Zucchini Apricot Jam

6 cups peeled and grated zucchini
1/4 cup water
1 1 3/4-ounce package powdered
   fruit pectin (Surejell or Penjell)
1/4 cup lemon juice

1 20-ounce can crushed pineapple,
   undrained
6 cups sugar
1 6-ounce package apricot gelatin
   (or 2 3-ounce packages)

Cook zucchini in the water for 15 minutes or until tender. Drain well. Stir in remaining ingredients with exception of gelatin. Boil 5 minutes. Stir in gelatin until dissolved. Spoon into sterilized jars and seal or top with paraffin. Process in boiling water bath for 10 minutes if desired. This jam also freezes well. Makes about 10 pints.

3. Grocery Stores and Lockers

In the 1940s and 1950s, most small towns in southwest Iowa had at least one grocery store/meat market that served the needs of rural customers. Many of these stores were family operations, with the husband, wife, and older children all pitching in to stock shelves, collect orders, deliver groceries, run the cash register, and keep the books. If there weren't enough family members to do everything, the owners hired neighbors and friends.

As a rule, the grocer doubled as the butcher, running the meat display at the back of the store and dispensing community news along with cuts of beef and pork. His wife, daughter, or daughter-in-law could often be found in a back room office using a hand-cranked adding machine to keep track of the bills rung up by customers whose credit was in good standing. Shoppers frequently charged their groceries for periods of up to four weeks and came into the store at the end of the month to pay their bills without being reminded.

The basic layout of most stores was similar. Sills inside the large front windows held displays of sale items, and the glass was often cluttered with posters announcing church suppers, auction sales, and school programs. Sunshine from the windows gleamed on the clean wooden

Cannon's Grocery-and-Lockers was located on the west side of the Sidney town square. The block also included a five-and-ten store, the Sidney Hotel, the Fremont County Savings Bank, and Penn Drug.

floorboards and provided light for the checker near the front of the stores. Customers entering the store could go up one aisle, turn at the back past the meat counter and ice cream freezer, then proceed down the other aisle to the cash register flanked with boxes of penny candy, cough drops, and gum.

Shopping was usually done by the farm women, the men coming to the grocery stores only in emergencies or to pick up an item or two. The women took their time in the aisles even though there was usually a clerk nearby to carry their baskets, to help them find a needed item, to fetch something off the top shelf, or to lift a can from a low area. It was a good time to visit with other shoppers, with the person at the cash register, and with the butcher slicing slabs of cured bacon and cutting thick pork chops from a loin. While the weekly newspapers of small towns carried a general account of local news, the real stories were shared from one person to the next in places like the grocery store.

When customers needed groceries delivered in town, they could telephone their wants to the store personnel. A clerk would fill the orders and deliver the goods to the customers' homes. A number of stores stocked trucks with groceries and sent them on weekly routes

For a time, Robert raised hogs with his brother-in-law, Oliver Bricker. This pure-bred, dark red duroc boar named Newcomer was a breeding boar that Robert fed, exercised, and groomed.

into the countryside to call on farm families. The convenience of these descendants of the old-time peddlers helped the business of the grocers and saved many a busy farm wife a trip to town when she needed staples such as flour, bacon, or sugar.

In the days before electric freezers were commonplace in homes, many grocers built lockers in the back of their stores and rented space in them to families with food to preserve. Freezing meats for long-time storage was easier for the country folks than using a hot stove to process jars of beef and pork and chicken. Asparagus, peas, strawberries, and many other vegetables and fruits also lent themselves well to freezing, retaining much of their flavor, texture, and nutritional value.

When we moved to the farm in 1948, we rented space in the locker at Cannon's Grocery in Robert's hometown of Sidney. His parents still lived there, and since we frequently drove the sixteen miles from our farm to visit them, it was easy for us to take along items to be placed in the locker.

The locker that Roy Cannon and his son, Malcom, had built in their store was a heavily insulated room banked with drawers and compartments identified with numbers and secured with locks. The metal drawers were roomy, about thirty-six inches long, twenty-five to thirty inches wide, and twenty-four inches deep. The compartments were like cupboards and were available in various sizes. A family could rent just the amount of space they needed, a drawer for ten dollars a month and a smaller compartment for eight dollars.

The temperature was kept at zero, but a smaller "fast freeze" room adjacent to the locker was even colder. The more quickly foods freeze the better they hold their flavor and texture. A customer could leave fresh foods with the Cannons who would mark the packages with the owner's name and locker number, put them on the shelves in the fast freeze room until they were frozen, then transfer them into the proper storage drawers and compartments. Their efforts made it possible for us to have meals with a fresh-from-the-garden flavor any time of year.

Pork Chow Mein

1 pound lean pork, cubed
2 cups hot water
2 cups sliced celery
1 cup chopped onion
1 sweet green pepper, diced
1 4-ounce can mushrooms, stems
  and pieces, undrained

1 small can pimientos
1 large can bean sprouts, drained
2 tablespoons soy sauce
2 tablespoons molasses
2 tablespoons cornstarch
3 tablespoons cold water

Brown pork pieces and then add hot water, cover, and simmer about 10 minutes. Add celery, onion, pepper, mushrooms, pimientos, and bean sprouts and continue simmering, stirring occasionally, for 12 to 15 minutes. To thicken, combine soy sauce, molasses, cornstarch, and cold water. Add to mixture in skillet and cook, stirring, until mixture bubbles and thickens. Serve over chow mein noodles. Serves 6 to 8.

Party Pork Chops

4 pork chops
2 cups water
1 tablespoon butter
1 onion, chopped
2 sweet green peppers, chopped
1/2 teaspoon onion salt
1 1-pound can whole peeled
   tomatoes, pureed

1 cup fresh chopped mushrooms
1/4 cup chopped parsley
1 teaspoon sugar
1/2 teaspoon black pepper
1/2 teaspoon chili powder
1/2 teaspoon oregano
2 cups chicken broth
1 tablespoon cornstarch

Simmer pork chops in water about 10 minutes. Remove from pan and place in large casserole, reserve the broth. Melt butter in large skillet and sauté onion and green peppers until tender. Add remaining ingredients with exception of cornstarch—including broth—and simmer for 15 minutes. Dissolve cornstarch in 2 tablespoons cold water, add, and continue cooking until mixture thickens. Remove sauce from fire and pour over the chops in the casserole. Cover and refrigerate several hours or overnight to blend flavors. Bake at 350 degrees for 20 to 25 minutes (or microwave for 10 to 12 minutes on medium high) until bubbly and heated through. Serve with hot cooked rice. This sauce and method are also excellent with chicken breasts. Freeze any leftover sauce to use later. Makes 4 generous servings.

Baked Pork Chops with Dressing

6 to 8 Iowa pork chops
1/3 cup butter or margarine,
   melted
2 cups bread crumbs
1 cup hot chicken broth

1 medium onion, finely chopped
3 stalks celery, finely chopped
1 teaspoon poultry seasoning or
   sage

Flour pork chops and brown in a small amount of cooking oil. Season with salt and pepper as desired and place in a baking dish. Combine remaining ingredients to make the dressing. Spoon a mound of dressing on top of each chop. Bake at 350 degrees for about 1 hour or until chops are cooked and dressing is brown. Makes 6 to 8 servings.

Elegant Pork Chops

MARINADE

2 cups soy sauce
1 cup water
1/2 cup brown sugar, packed

1 tablespoon molasses
1/2 teaspoon salt

Combine ingredients and pour over 6 Iowa or America-cut pork chops. Marinate several hours or overnight. Lift chops out of marinade and place in a 9-by-13-inch pan and bake, uncovered, in a 350-degree oven while you prepare the topping.

TOPPING

1/3 cup water
1 14-ounce bottle catsup
1 12-ounce bottle chili sauce

1/2 cup brown sugar, packed
1 tablespoon dry mustard

Combine ingredients and bring to a boil. Pour over chops. Cover pan with foil and continue baking at 350 degrees until done, turning several times. This takes about 1 hour, depending on the thickness of the chops. The leftover marinade and the topping can be individually brought to a boil and poured into fruit or freezer jars and refrigerated or frozen to use another time. Makes 6 servings.

Delicious Pork Casserole

1 pound ground pork
1/4 cup chopped onion

1/4 cup diced sweet green pepper
   (optional)

2 cups diced celery
1 cup cooked rice or cooked
   macaroni
1 1-ounce package beef noodle soup
   mix

1 1-ounce package onion soup mix
2 cups hot water
1 4-ounce can mushrooms, stems
   and pieces, undrained
1/2 cup toasted almonds

In a skillet combine the ground pork, onion, green pepper, and celery. Cover and cook on low heat for 30 minutes, stirring occasionally to be sure mixture doesn't stick. Drain off excess fat. Stir rice or macaroni and soup mixes into hot water and add with remaining ingredients to skillet. Spoon into casserole and bake at 350 degrees for about 1 hour. This recipe freezes very well. Remove from freezer and bake according to directions or cook in the microwave for 15 to 20 minutes after thawing. Makes 6 to 8 servings.

Honey Fruited Ham

1 whole precooked ham
12 whole cloves
1/2 cup vinegar
2 cups pickled peach juice
1 cup honey

1 cup brown sugar, packed
1 cup diced oranges
1 cup pineapple chunks
1 cup white grapes

Lay the ham in a roaster. Stick the cloves in the meat. Combine the vinegar and peach juice and pour over ham. Smooth the honey over the top and then press in the brown sugar. Bake at 300 degrees, uncovered, for 30 minutes. Cover and bake, basting every 20 minutes, until tender and heated through. Add the oranges, cover, and continue baking for another 20 minutes. Slice and arrange meat on a platter with the pineapple and grapes around it. This is a large recipe, but it is easy to cut down for a smaller portion of ham.

4. Chickens

~~~~~~~~~~~~~~~~~~~~

It's a wonder anyone makes the effort to raise chickens, for they seem to be born with no instinct at all. They do not know how to drink or how to pick up their food. They must be shown how to do both by either a mother hen or a patient surrogate human parent or they die. Chickens don't know how to come in out of the rain and, if they get wet, they may catch their death of cold.

Chickens are easily frightened. The sound of a coyote or a rat prowling around outside a chicken house can send them scurrying hysterically into a corner where they pile on top of each other. If the chickens get cold they frequently bunch up to keep warm, and those on the bottom may smother.

Several hundred baby chicks peeping noisily can aggravate truckers, post office personnel, and hatchery workers. A flock of laying hens can cause a racket just with their normal cackling, but let trouble come near the pens and they set up a cacophony of squawking that brings everyone running to their aid. Many farmers keep a rooster just because they like the sound of its crowing a loud "cock-a-doodle-do" at first light.

Despite all the hazards of caring for poultry, the ease of cooking taste-tempting dishes made from eggs or chickens overcame any reluctance on my part to raise the birds. Each spring we lived on the farm I would buy one hundred baby chicks, enough for our year's supply of meat. I did not have to order our chickens by mail as some rural people did since we lived near enough to the towns of Hamburg and Shenandoah to pick up the chicks from their hatcheries. I would telephone in the number of chickens I wanted and ask when a hatch would be ready.

Left on their own, hens lay eggs in nests, sit on them for twenty-one days, turn them once in a while with their beaks and feet, and fluff out their maternal feathers to keep the growing embryos warm. Once the chicks peck their way out of the shells, the mother hen guides them in the ways of eating and drinking and running around catching bugs. Even though most chicks look alike, each mother hen can identify her own chicks, and she has her own soft clucking sound which helps each chick recognize its mother.

During World War II, the price of eggs and chickens increased as meat became scarce and the demand for chickens grew. Farm women in the Midwest raised larger flocks of chickens for their own cooking and to sell to earn needed income. The commercial hatcheries with their mechanical incubators enjoyed a boom as they provided more and more hatched baby chicks than the hens could produce on home nests.

By the middle of the century, the city of Shenandoah thirteen miles from our farm had six commercial hatcheries. One hatchery reportedly kept as many as 100,000 hens busy laying eggs for their banks of incubator drawers. The hatching times were staggered so that approximately 20,000 chicks were hatched each day in just that one plant. During the spring hatching season, hatcheries in southwest Iowa sent out thousands of chicks a day to customers on farms and in small towns.

If buyers wanted all female chickens to grow into hens to lay eggs or all roosters to raise as fryers or to replace old roosters in their flocks of setting hens, they would buy chickens which had been "sexed." The technique for identifying male and female chicks was discovered by the Japanese, and the most highly trained and efficient sexers were men of that ethnic background. They came into southwest Iowa in the spring,

The interior of Mayway Hatchery in Shenandoah. Edward May, Sr., photo.

quietly did their work, and then, when the hatching season was over, vanished back to wherever they came from. We didn't know much about where they stayed or what they did in their spare time. Except for one or two of the single men, socializing with local residents was not part of their lives, and vice versa. In fact, socializing with anyone very different from themselves was not part of most rural Iowans' daily lives.

During the war years, the Japanese workers disappeared into the Japanese-American units in the army, such as Iowa's 34th Rainbow Division, or into detention camps. Following the war, these specialists returned and, in their unobtrusive way, continued doing the work of sexing chickens.

The process of determining male from female chicks is difficult, since the reproductive organs of both are internal. A technician would pick up a freshly hatched chick and gently press out any residual egg yolk which had not been absorbed by the chick for food as it grew in

As Bob Troxel and his son, Tom, watch, workers at the Hamburg Hatchery load boxes of baby chicks onto a railroad car to ship to customers all over the Midwest. Bob Troxel photo.

the shell. The worker would then turn back each chick's vent far enough to see the internal male organs, if present, to identify the males, or the lack of such organs to identify the females. A few chickens like Barred Rocks and Rhode Island Reds had identifiable markings and colors, so the sexers could tell by outward appearance which would become cockerels (young roosters) and which would become pullets (young hens). Once the chicks were identified and sorted, they were boxed and shipped by parcel post or railway express to customers.

The "straight runs" or unsexed chickens I always bought were cheaper and served our purposes just fine. We only needed a few laying hens for our egg supply, and the rest, cockerels and pullets alike, were eventually turned into meat pies and stews and sandwiches.

While some of the women cared for large flocks of laying hens and sold eggs to the hatcheries, it was more common for a farm wife to work with smaller numbers of poultry. She'd buy 200 to 500 baby chicks each spring, feed them for about thirteen weeks until they reached fryer size, then dress them out to sell. For only seventy-five cents, a town woman could buy a farm-raised, corn-fed, fresh-dressed chicken delivered to her door.

If she wanted to keep only a few laying hens, a farm wife could sell extra eggs to regular customers or to the produce houses in town which purchased them for resale. She could also trade the extra eggs at the grocery store for food. Sometimes the amount of groceries a family bought to eat during a week depended on how many eggs the hens had laid.

Other families, like ours, raised just enough chicks to provide meat and eggs for their own use—usually one hundred. Once we had ordered the chicks we needed, Robert and I headed for the chicken house to get it prepared for its new occupants. We scrubbed the floor, then Robert partitioned off a small area with boards to create a nursery and hung an extension cord with a heat lamp overhead to provide warmth. I scattered finely ground corn on the floor, then filled several one-quart fruit jars with water and screwed them into shallow metal water dispensers. When I turned the jars upside down, a little of the water ran into the saucerlike bases. The dispenser had openings just wide enough for the chicks to get their tiny beaks inside.

The day-old chicks were packaged in cardboard boxes about thirty inches square that were divided into four sections. Twenty-five chicks fit into each compartment. The bottoms of the boxes were sprinkled with shredded wood shavings, known as excelsior, to protect the chicks during transport and to provide litter for their droppings.

Our children always enjoyed climbing into the pickup and riding along to the hatchery to get the chicks, and they mimicked the peep-peeping of the tiny creatures all the way home. Most of all, they liked to lift the fluffy yellow creatures out of the box and put them under the warmth of the lamp in the chicken house. I'd show them how to hold the tiny bodies gently, how to dip the baby beaks in the waterers to get a first sip, and how to press the beaks into some of the ground grain on the floor so the chicks would learn how to eat.

Fortunately, as the chicks grew larger they also became less interesting. The cuddly bits of fluff turned into gangly young hens and pompous feisty roosters who made their dominating presence known around the chicken yard. By the time the chickens were large enough to use as broilers or fryers, the children had lost interest and were off playing with the baby pigs in the hog house, the new calf in the pasture, and the kittens and puppies in the barn.

By the end of summer, half the chickens had become entrees for hearty meals, and those that were left were the size we liked to roast, stew, or fry for winter meals. When the garden stopped producing vegetables and fruits for canning or freezing, we set aside several days to butcher the remaining chickens and prepare the meat for the locker. My mother, whom we all called Grandma Corrie, would come from her home in Shenandoah to assist. I prized her cheerful help and her companionship during those long workdays.

Robert began the operation by building a big fire at one side of the nearby hog lot. He put a washtub full of water on a grate over the fire. While the water heated, he and the children went into the chicken yard with long wires hooked at one end and used them to snare the legs of the squawking birds. He grabbed the chickens by their legs, put them into a covered crate, and carried them to a place near the fire. He took each chicken, placed its head on the ground, and lay a broom handle over its thin neck. With his feet firmly set on top of the stick, he gave a quick pull on the chicken's legs, then tossed the headless bird onto the grass where it would flop for a few moments in a macabre dance as the next chicken met the same fate. No wonder the rural folks said a person acting erratically was "like a chicken with its head off."

Robert dipped each headless chicken in the boiling water to loosen the feathers, then plucked them out. Even with a cool October breeze blowing, the heat from the flames, the steam from the boiling water, and the constant effort as he pulled and tugged caused Robert's face and arms to glisten with sweat. The air stank with the odor of wet feathers and the smell of wood smoke.

The children carried the plucked chickens up to the house where Grandma Corrie and I took over. We held the defeathered carcasses over the gas flame of the kitchen stove to singe off any hairs, then washed each chicken, scraped the skin with a knife, pulled out any remaining pin feathers, and gutted and cut up most of the birds. We left a few large ones whole to use for roasting or stewing.

The children were fascinated with the entire procedure. When they weren't running back and forth bringing more chickens from the hog lot gate to the kitchen, they were up on chairs watching Grandma Corrie and me dressing the fowls. It was an impromptu lesson in basic anatomy.

As the hours passed, the piles of chicken legs and thighs and giblets grew high in the pans of salt water we used to leech out any blood remaining in the meat. Robert came in now and then to get the pail of entrails and threw them out to the hogs.

While we worked, I stewed up enough bony pieces to make creamed chicken on toast for a quick noon meal. It was important to keep my crew of helpers fed and happy. If we were fortunate, Grandma Corrie would reminisce about the way she used to catch and dress a chicken and fry it when unexpected company arrived. "It was good fresh meat, especially in the summer since we had no refrigeration. As a form of invitation to dinner, I've even heard ladies say 'come over and we'll kill a chicken.'"

There was not much time to sit at the table and visit for, as was true with most of the tasks on a farm, once we started butchering chickens, we had to keep working until the job was finished. Our backs ached from bending over the sink washing and cutting. Our hands grew raw from the sharp bones and pin feathers. Our fingers wrinkled up like prunes from the long hours in the water, but we continued until the quota we had set for the day was reached. Thirty-five chickens were the most we three adults and two children managed to dress out in one day.

When we had the meat wrapped in freezer paper and packed into dishpans and roasters, we loaded it into the pickup and drove to Sidney to deliver it to the locker. Roy or Malcom Cannon marked the packages of chickens with our name and locker number, fast froze each one, and stored them in our drawer until we needed them for winter meals.

Many people know how delicious fried chicken is, but not everyone knows the steps it takes to get it from the egg to the table. I knew little of the process until I moved to the farm and experienced firsthand the work involved. Even though I found little inspiration from the work, when one of those farm-raised chickens was fried or roasted to a tender brown finish and served with fluffy mashed potatoes topped with rich, yellow chicken gravy, the feast was well worth the effort.

Creamed Chicken on Toast

1 cup diced cooked chicken
2 tablespoons butter or margarine
2 tablespoons flour

1 cup milk
salt and pepper to taste
toast

Cut cooked chicken into bite-sized pieces. Melt butter or margarine and blend in flour, stirring until smooth and bubbly. Gradually stir in milk and continue cooking, stirring, until thick. Add chicken and season as desired. Serve over toast. Serves 2 to 4.

Oven-Fried Chicken

1 fryer, cut up
1 cup milk
1 cup flour
1/2 teaspoon salt

1/2 teaspoon pepper
1 teaspoon paprika
1/2 cup butter or oil

Rinse and pat pieces of chicken dry, soak in milk for about 5 minutes. Lift out of milk and shake off excess. Combine dry ingredients in paper or plastic sack and shake chicken in the sack a few pieces at a time. Heat butter or oil in a shallow baking pan. Place pieces of chicken in the butter or oil, skin-side down. Bake for 30 minutes at 350 degrees. Turn pieces over and continue baking for 15 more minutes or until done on all sides and golden brown. For skillet-fried chicken, the same technique can be followed except the pieces of chicken are cooked in a skillet on top of the stove with shortening about 1 inch deep. Turn frequently until pieces are nicely brown and cooked through—about 40 minutes. Serves up to 6, depending on size of chicken.

Apricot Chicken

2 3-pound chickens, cut up
1 1-ounce package onion soup mix
1 cup apricot jam or preserves
1 cup creamy Thousand Island
  dressing (or Russian dressing)

Put chicken pieces in shallow, greased baking pan, skin-side up. Combine remaining ingredients and brush sauce over top. Bake in a 350-degree oven uncovered for 1 hour or until chicken is done, basting often with remaining sauce. Turn at least once. Serves about 10.

Magnificent Chicken Pie

1 stewing chicken (or large fryer)
6 tablespoons butter or margarine
12 small onions
7 tablespoons flour
salt and pepper to taste
dash of mace
1/2 teaspoon Worcestershire sauce
1 cup milk or half-and-half
2 cups chicken broth

Cover chicken with water and simmer, covered, until tender, 1 to 2 hours. Cool. Remove skin and bones and cut meat into bite-sized pieces. Place in 9-by-13-inch baking pan. In a skillet, sauté onions in butter or margarine. With a slotted spoon, lift onions from skillet and spoon over the chicken. Blend flour into drippings in skillet, add seasonings and Worcestershire sauce and gradually stir in milk or half-

and-half and chicken broth. Cook, stirring, until mixture is thickened. Pour gravy over chicken and onion layers. Put in a 400-degree oven to keep hot while you prepare the biscuits. Makes about 8 servings.

Carrot Biscuits

2 cups biscuit mix (or make your
  own—see recipe below)

1/2 cup coarsely grated raw carrots
milk to make a soft dough

Combine ingredients. Roll out the dough and cut into rings with a doughnut cutter so each biscuit has a hole in the center. If you want larger biscuits or don't have a doughnut cutter, use a can as a cutter for the circle and a lid from a catsup or other bottle to make the center hole. Arrange biscuit rings on top of the chicken in the casserole. Brush tops with milk. Bake 15 to 20 minutes at 425 degrees or until light brown. Meanwhile, cook 1 cup of fresh peas or 1 package of frozen peas with a little water added or heat 1 can of peas. Drain. Season the peas and put a heaping spoonful in the center of each biscuit ring. Any remaining peas can be served in a separate dish.

Real Country Biscuits

2 cups flour
3/4 teaspoon salt
1 tablespoon baking powder

1/4 cup shortening
1/4 teaspoon baking soda
1 cup buttermilk

Sift first three ingredients into bowl. Cut in shortening until mixture is like coarse bread crumbs. (Lard makes light, tender biscuits just as it does pie crust, but homogenized shortening like Crisco is also excellent.) Combine baking soda with buttermilk. Blend into dry ingredients with fork. When barely moistened, turn out on floured breadboard and knead a few times. Pat out to about 1/2 inch thick and cut into rounds. Bake on greased cookie sheet at 425 degrees for 10 to 12 minutes or until brown. This is a fine recipe to use with Carrot Biscuit recipe. Makes about 1 dozen biscuits, depending on size.

Chicken with Rice and Carrots

1/2 cup uncooked brown or white
   rice
1 tablespoon olive oil
2 uncooked boneless chicken
   breasts, diced
1/4 cup white wine
1 cup chicken broth

2 carrots, sliced
6 green onions, sliced
1/4 cup chopped peanuts
1 teaspoon cornstarch
1 tablespoon cold water
1 tablespoon soy sauce
salt and pepper to taste

Cook rice in boiling salted water until tender. Set aside. Sauté chicken breasts in hot oil until cooked through. Remove chicken from skillet and stir in wine, broth, and carrots and cook for 5 minutes. Add onions and continue cooking until vegetables are tender. Add chicken, peanuts and seasonings. Continue cooking until carrots are tender. Dissolve cornstarch in water and soy sauce, add to broth, and continue cooking, stirring, until mixture thickens slightly. Spoon chicken mixture over hot rice. Makes 2 servings.

Honey Chicken Wings

3 pounds chicken wings
salt and pepper to taste
2 tablespoons vegetable oil
1/2 cup soy sauce

2 tablespoons catsup
3/4 cup honey
1/2 clove garlic, minced

Cut off wing tips of chicken and discard or save to use later in soup. Cut remaining wings into two pieces. Sprinkle with salt and pepper and place in baking pan. Combine remaining ingredients and pour over wings. Bake at 350 degrees for 30 or 40 minutes, turning once or twice, until wings are done and sauce is thickened. These can be served as appetizers or as a main dish or for a buffet dinner. How many this recipe serves depends on how hungry the diners are and what else is on the menu.

Stewed Chicken and Noodles

1 chicken
salt to taste
2 tablespoons chopped parsley

1/4 teaspoon celery seeds
1 onion, diced

Use a stewing chicken if possible or a large fryer if not. Cut into pieces, cover with water. Add remaining ingredients and simmer until meat is tender (or cook in pressure pan for about 20 minutes at 10 pounds pressure). Strain broth and return to kettle. Taste broth and add more seasonings if desired. Remove chicken meat from bone, cut into bite-sized pieces, and set aside. Prepare noodles and cook in broth as directed. Serves 6 to 8.

Homemade Noodles

2 cups flour
1/2 teaspoon baking powder
2 eggs

2 tablespoons half-and-half or milk
1/2 teaspoon butter

Combine flour and baking powder in a bowl. Make a well in the center and add remaining ingredients. Mix with a fork (or fingers) until ingredients are well blended. Roll on a floured board as thinly as possible. Let dry for at least 20 minutes, turning once. Roll up like a jelly roll and cut into narrow strips. Shake and separate noodles on breadboard.

Cover with a clean tea towel and let dry for 2 or more hours. Drop into hot, seasoned chicken broth and simmer for about 10 minutes or until tender. Return chicken meat to broth and serve hot. The noodles are not salted but the broth is, which helps keep the noodles tender. Noodles can be made ahead and, after the drying time is over, slipped into plastic bags, and frozen until time to pop them into the broth to cook. This recipe can also be used in the pasta-making machines. After combining ingredients, knead several times and then cut into portions to fit into machine. Run each portion through the cutter as directed, separate noodles, and cover with a clean tea towel. Continue as directed. Serves 6 to 8.

Chicken Tetrazzini

1/2 pound spaghetti	paprika
1/2 to 1 cup fresh mushrooms, sliced (or 1 4-ounce can mushrooms, stems and pieces, drained)	1/4 teaspoon pepper
	1/8 teaspoon nutmeg
	1/4 teaspoon Worcestershire sauce
	2 tablespoons flour
3 tablespoons butter or margarine	3 tablespoons butter or margarine
1 tablespoon lemon juice	1 cup cream, half-and-half, or milk
2 to 3 cups diced cooked chicken	2/3 cup grated Parmesan cheese

Cook spaghetti in salted boiling water or in diluted chicken broth. Drain and place in bottom of baking dish. Sauté mushrooms in 3 tablespoons butter or margarine—do not brown—sprinkle with lemon juice and a dash of salt. Make a layer of the mushrooms over the top of the spaghetti. Make a layer of cooked chicken over the mushrooms. Blend together the seasonings, Worcestershire sauce, flour, and 3 tablespoons butter or margarine and cook, stirring, until smooth and bubbly. Add cream (or half-and-half or milk) and continue to cook and stir until thick. Pour gravy over chicken. Top with cheese. Cover and refrigerate until time to bake. Bake at 400 degrees for 25 minutes or until heated through. Freezes well. Serves 6 to 8.

Chicken with Sour Cream Sauce

4 chicken breasts
1/3 cup flour
1/2 teaspoon salt
1/4 teaspoon pepper
1/2 teaspoon paprika
1/4 cup butter or margarine
3/4 cup white wine or water
1 teaspoon chicken bouillon
   granules

1 cup sliced mushrooms (or 1
   4-ounce can mushrooms,
   drained)
1/2 cup sliced onion
1/2 cup diced carrot
1/2 cup diced celery
1/2 cup sour cream

In a paper or plastic sack combine flour, salt, pepper, and paprika. Shake chicken breasts in flour mixture to coat. Melt 2 tablespoons butter or margarine in frying pan. Brown chicken breasts on both sides, remove from skillet, and set aside. Add remaining butter to skillet, stir in remaining flour mixture, and stir until smooth and bubbly. Add wine or water and stir until smooth. Add bouillon, mushrooms, and vegetables. Return chicken breasts to mixture, cover, and simmer for about 25 minutes or until vegetables are tender and chicken is done. Remove chicken to serving plate and add sour cream gradually to sauce in pan. Heat just to scalding but do not boil so cream does not separate. Pour sauce over chicken. Makes 4 servings.

Plum-Glazed Baked Chicken

1 whole fryer
seasonings to taste
1/4 cup water
1/4 cup soy sauce

2 tablespoons honey
1/2 cup plum jelly
2 teaspoons vinegar

Season chicken with salt, pepper, a little ginger, and cinnamon as desired. Place in baking pan with 1/4 cup water in bottom of pan and cover with foil. Bake at 350 degrees for about 30 minutes, basting at least once with drippings. Combine remaining ingredients and brush on chicken. Bake 15 minutes covered with foil, then remove foil and continue baking and basting until brown and glazed. Serves 4 to 6.

5. The Beef Club

~~~~~~

B efore the time when electricity made refrigerators a possibility in rural homes, keeping meat from spoiling in the heat of summer was a constant problem for farm families. If a farmer took a steer from the herd and butchered it, the 400 to 500 pounds of meat would be far more than one family could eat before the bulk of the meat spoiled. Farmers might be able to sell some beef to their neighbors and to families in town, but a week later their own families would be without fresh meat again.

That's why, in the late 1800s, farmers in our part of the country began joining together to form beef clubs. Each club member was responsible for donating one steer per year for the entire group. From late spring until late autumn, the timing of the donations was scheduled so that a steer would be butchered each week and the cuts of meat divided among the families that made up the club. Every steer had to meet quality and weight standards set by the farmers. If the animal was larger than expected, its owner got to keep the extra meat. If it was underweight, the donating farmer paid the difference.

Even after electricity and refrigerators came to our farms, the idea of the beef club was so practical and so much a part of everyday life that many of the clubs lived on well into the 1950s. The club we belonged

This 1910 photo shows the men of the West Point Beef Club lined up outside the barn as they gathered to pick up their cuts of meat. Don Rorebeck photo.

to, the Fairview Beef Club, had been formed in 1909 and was named after a one-room country schoolhouse that the children of many of the early farm families had attended. If our club had a clubhouse, it was the barn of our neighbor to the east, Boyd Hamilton, Sr. A section of the Hamiltons' barn was equipped with electricity, water, and a floor drain, which made it an excellent place to use as a slaughterhouse.

Every Wednesday during the warm months, a butcher named Ben Darby would sharpen up his knives and bring them out to the Hamiltons' barn to turn that week's beef club steer into steaks and roasts. Ben would kill the steer late in the afternoon, skin and eviscerate it, and let it hang for a bit to bleed out well and firm before he cut it up. He weighed out the portions for each family, covered the meat with clean cloths, and let it cool until morning.

The Hamilton family provided Ben with a room and meals while he was butchering for our club. The rest of the week he drove across the country from one beef club to another, butchering their steers and enjoying their hospitality. In seven days he would be back at the Hamiltons' barn, ready to dismantle the Fairview Beef Club's next steer.

Every Thursday morning before dawn, while the air was still and

The early beef club facilities were more primitive than those that came later. Two butchers, circa 1910, wait for the farmers to arrive to get their portions of fresh meat. Don Rorebeck photo.

cool, Robert would drive his pickup the four miles to the Hamilton farm to pick up our portion of meat. Since we were a small family of four, we needed only a half share. Our friend Myron Reese was also a half member, and together our two families provided one steer to the club each year.

A full share of meat consisted of fourteen pounds of various cuts and a few extra pieces good to put into stews or to crank by hand through a grinder to make hamburger. While some of the farmers carried home their portions of meat in clean white cloth feed sacks, Robert would put our half share of seven pounds into a dishpan and cover it with a tea towel for the drive back to our farm. When he arrived, I liked to fry a piece of fresh steak along with eggs collected that morning and serve them with toast made from homemade bread for our breakfast.

After breakfast, I'd use my kitchen scales to weigh out and ration the meat. About two pounds would be enough for the recipes I was planning for the family during the week. I put the pieces into the small plastic bags that had just come on the market and stored them in the refrigerator, then wrapped the rest of the meat in freezer paper and took it to town to the locker at Cannon's grocery. Along with the chickens, plus a hog and a lamb that we had the Cannons butcher for us and put in the locker, the beef would see us through the months of the year when the club was not in operation.

Since farmers tried to outdo one another in producing the best corn-fed steer for the club, rural families often had beef that was especially succulent, tender, and full of flavor. The beef clubs and lockers made it possible for meat to be a part of farm meals throughout the year. It is not surprising that with ingredients of such quality, the recipes containing beef were mouth-watering good.

Stockyard Stew

5 pounds beef shank with bone (or
  3 pounds stewing beef)
2 quarts water
1 clove garlic, minced
1 teaspoon salt
1/3 cup uncooked barley or rice
1/2 cup chopped celery tops
2 cups chopped onions
2 to 3 cups tomatoes

1/3 cup butter
1 1/2 cups chopped celery
1 cup diced carrots
1 cup green beans
1 cup diced potatoes
1 cup coarsely chopped cabbage
2 cups fresh or frozen peas
salt and pepper to taste

Brown meat in a small amount of shortening. Cover with water, add garlic, salt, barley or rice, celery tops, and onions. Simmer 1 hour or so until meat is tender (or cook in pressure pan at 10 pounds pressure for 20 minutes). Skim fat from top of soup. (Chilling makes this easy.) Remove meat from shank bones, cut into bite-sized pieces, discard bones. Add vegetables to the broth and simmer for about 20 minutes or until tender. Return meat to broth. Season as desired. The Stockyard

Inn in Omaha was a restaurant where the farmers liked to eat when they took a load of hogs or cattle to market. This stew is similar to the specialty of the Inn. Makes about 10 servings.

Curried Beef and Rice

3 pounds stewing beef
salt and pepper to taste
2 large onions, diced
1 small sweet green pepper, diced
2 cups canned or fresh tomatoes
1 teaspoon curry powder

1 tablespoon vinegar
1 tablespoon apricot jam
4 or 5 potatoes, peeled and diced
1 tablespoon cornstarch
1 tablespoon cold water

Brown meat in a little cooking oil. Cover with water, add salt and pepper, and simmer slowly until tender. While this is cooking, brown diced onions and green pepper in small amount of oil, stir in tomatoes. Combine curry powder with vinegar, stir in apricot jam until smooth. Add to fried onion mixture and then add to meat and broth along with the potatoes. Continue simmering until potatoes are tender. Blend cornstarch and cold water until smooth, stir into broth, and simmer, stirring, until thick. Serve over hot cooked rice. This dish is delicious served with bananas, coconut, and chutney. Makes about 10 servings.

Pepper Steak

1/2 cup butter or margarine
2 pounds round steak, cut into thin
   strips
1/4 teaspoon garlic powder
1/2 cup chopped onion
2 sweet green peppers, sliced
2 cups canned or fresh tomatoes

1 beef bouillon cube (or 1 teaspoon
   granules)
1 tablespoon cornstarch
1/4 cup water
3 tablespoons soy sauce
1 teaspoon sugar

Melt butter in skillet. Add steak and garlic powder. Brown. Remove meat and add onion and green peppers to shortening in the skillet and brown for 2 minutes. Add meat, tomatoes, and bouillon. Simmer 5 minutes. Blend cornstarch, water, soy sauce, and sugar, add to mixture in skillet. Cook, stirring, until thickened. A little more water can be added if needed. Serve piping hot over hot cooked rice. Ingredients can be prepared ahead of time and refrigerated to cook just before time to serve. Serves 6 to 8.

Farmer's Stew

2 pounds stew meat
2 cups hot water
1 teaspoon Worcestershire sauce
1 clove garlic, minced
1 medium onion, sliced
2 small bay leaves

salt and pepper to taste
pinch of allspice
1 teaspoon sugar
6 carrots, halved
8 small onions
3 or 4 big potatoes, quartered

Combine all but last three ingredients and cook in pressure pan at 10 pounds pressure for 20 minutes. Run cold water over cooker and when pressure pan has cooled, open the lid and add carrots, small onions, and potatoes. Bring the pressure back up to 10 pounds and cook for 3 minutes. Thicken broth with flour and water if desired. This can also be cooked in a stewing kettle for 1 hour or until the meat is tender and then for 20 more minutes after the vegetables are added. Makes 6 to 8 servings.

Country Meat Loaf

1 pound ground beef
1/2 pound ground pork
1 medium onion, chopped fine
1 medium potato, peeled and
   chopped fine

1/2 cup uncooked rolled oats
2 eggs
salt and pepper to taste

Combine ingredients, shape into a loaf, and place in a greased baking pan. Bake at 350 degrees for 30 minutes. Drain off fat. Then top with Meat Loaf Topping. One loaf serves 6.

MEAT LOAF TOPPING

1 tablespoon butter or margarine	1/4 cup catsup
1 tablespoon flour	2 tablespoons brown sugar, packed
1 cup tomato juice	(optional)

Stir flour into melted butter or margarine. Add remaining ingredients and pour over meat loaf. Return to oven and continue cooking at 350 degrees for 20 more minutes. This recipe freezes well either baked or unbaked. It can easily be doubled for two loaves.

Porcupine Meat Balls

1 pound ground beef	1/3 cup uncooked rice
1/2 pound ground pork	salt and pepper to taste
1 medium-sized onion, chopped	1 10 3/4-ounce can tomato soup
1 sweet green pepper, chopped	1/2 cup water
(optional)	

Mix all ingredients together with exception of the last two. Shape into meatballs and brown thoroughly in a little shortening. Combine tomato soup and water and pour over meatballs. Cover tightly and simmer for about 45 minutes to 1 hour or until meatballs are done and rice is tender. Add a little more water if needed. These are called porcupine meat balls because the rice looks like little quills. Serves 5 or 6.

Favorite Spaghetti

2 tablespoons oil
2 medium onions, diced
2 pounds ground beef
2 8-ounce cans tomato paste
3 cups water
1 10 1/2-ounce can tomato soup
1 1/2 teaspoons oregano

1/4 teaspoon sweet basil leaves
1/8 teaspoon marjoram
salt and pepper to taste
3 cloves garlic, crushed
1 4-ounce can mushrooms, stems
   and pieces, undrained
1/4 cup grated Parmesan cheese

Heat the oil in a large, heavy skillet. Brown onions until golden. Stir in the ground beef and continue cooking until nicely brown. Add tomato paste, water, and tomato soup. Cover and simmer slowly for about 2 hours. Add a little more water if needed. Stir in seasonings, garlic, and mushrooms and continue cooking another 20 minutes. Just before serving add the cheese. Serve over hot, cooked spaghetti. Sauce freezes well. Makes at least 10 servings.

Easy Ground Beef Dinner

2 pounds ground beef
2 cups water, more if needed
2 beef bouillon cubes

salt and pepper to taste
rice
1 to 2 1-pound cans peas

Brown ground beef in a little shortening. Drain off fat. Add water and bouillon cubes, stir to blend, cover, and let simmer while the rice cooks. Add more water if needed to keep meat mixture moist. Cook enough rice for 4 servings. Heat peas until bubbly. To serve, put a mound of fluffy hot rice on each plate and make a depression in the center. Spoon on the ground beef mixture and liquid. Drain the peas and spoon over the rice-beef layers. This makes a good cookout menu. Serves 4.

6. Milking

~~~~~~~~~~~~~~~~~~~~~~~~~~~

It did not take Robert long to discover what all the long-time farmers knew: he could not make enough from the sale of crops, hay, and livestock from our small rented farm to support his family. Soon after we moved to Cottonwood Farm, Robert went to town to buy milk cows. He arranged verbally for a bank loan, then drove to the sale barn where farmers came to auction off livestock. He purchased eleven good, gentle Guernseys and brought them home to add to the milk cow we already owned. Once he had purchased the cows, he returned to the bank and signed the loan papers, now completed with the amount he paid and with the cows listed as collateral.

Milking a dozen cows by hand was a time-consuming task that had to be done every day, morning and evening, regardless of what other tasks were waiting. Cows which were not milked regularly would stop producing milk—"Go dry," the farmers called it. When electricity came to rural areas, many farmers purchased milking machines to ease the work. The equipment was too expensive for us, but Robert insisted he did not mind milking by hand. "It's quiet in the barn," he said. "I just rest my head on a cow's flank, relax, and think." And he did make milking look easy. He'd balance on a one-legged stool, grasp a teat in

A 1951 bill for a machinery and livestock sale similar to the one where Robert purchased our milk cows. Shenandoah Evening Sentinel.

each hand, squeeze and pull, squeeze and pull. The milk struck the side of the pail with a rhythmic cadence that was almost hypnotic.

The cats came by during the milking, for they knew that Robert would fill the old bread pan near the door with fresh, warm milk. If a cat sat near enough while he was milking, Robert would direct a squirt into its mouth, sending the cat into a spasm of delight and a session of licking its fur for spattered drops which lasted almost as long as the milking itself.

I never did learn to milk, but when I could get away from my own chores in the kitchen and garden, I would take the children and go out to the barn where we would sit on upturned buckets with our backs against the wooden boards of the barn and watch Robert milk. If the children grew bored with much sitting, they'd often urge me to climb up into the haymow to look for a new litter of kittens. By the time we found them, Robert would be finished, and we'd trudge back to the house carrying the buckets filled with milk ready to be separated.

In 1877, Gustav de Laval of Sweden invented a machine that would separate the cream from the whole milk. In 1948, we had a de Laval separator on our back porch that worked on the same principle of centrifugal force as had the original machine seventy years earlier. It consisted of a large round tank, a rotating bowl, a set of discs, a cream outlet, and a milk outlet. The bowl of the early machines had been spun with a hand crank. Our separator had an electric motor.

I always put a pitcher of strained, fresh whole milk in the refrigerator for our family's use, then took the rest of the milk to the porch to separate. When I switched on the motor, the separator bowl started turning with a soft whine which rapidly became shrill and high-pitched as it reached full speed. That was my signal to pour the whole milk through a strainer and into the separator. The cream spun toward the top of the bowl and out a spout into a cream can while the skimmed milk was thrown downward through another spout where it poured into a bucket.

We kept our cans of cream cool in the cave until the produce truck arrived once a week to collect them. The driver had a regular route around the countryside picking up eggs, chickens, and cream that he delivered to the local creamery/produce house. Robert fed the leftover skimmed milk to the hogs.

When the separating was completed, I washed every section of the equipment which had been touched by the milk and cream since any residue could sour the next batch of milk. It took at least twenty minutes to do this, and I never met a person who didn't consider washing the cream separator one of the most disliked tasks on the farm.

Whenever I needed butter, I churned some from the fresh cream. At first I put the cream into a gallon mason jar, screwed on the lid, and shook the jar until the lumps of butter "came." Later, I bought a Daisy churn—a gallon rectangular glass jar with wooden paddles fastened to a handle on top that I turned by hand. Occasionally, I used my electric mixer to whip a smaller amount of cream into butter.

I washed the butter and "worked it"—kneading it well to get out the buttermilk—put it in a covered bowl in the refrigerator, and brought it out to spread on hot homemade bread or to float in golden puddles on top of fluffy mountains of mashed potatoes. The fresh buttermilk left from making the butter had a sharp, tangy flavor that I liked for drinking and cooking.

Providing our family with dairy products was not just a matter of spending an hour or more each morning and evening milking the cows and caring for the milk and cream. It also meant keeping the animals healthy and well fed. It meant herding them out to the pasture in the morning and bringing them in at night.

Robert usually did these tasks, but when he was away helping the neighbors put up hay or pick corn, I brought in the milk cows. With the children trotting by my side, I would walk to the pasture through the small timber which edged a clear, sparkling, spring-fed brook. Unfortunately, my pleasure with the lovely view evaporated as soon as the cows saw me. The moment I appeared they hightailed it as far away as the fence would allow. Most of them would eventually give in to my pleadings and head through the gate, but not the cow we called Ada. When the rest of the herd was at the bottom of the hill she was at the top. When they were ambling through the gate, she was running off in the other direction. I would chase her around and around the

Farm dogs like Sparkle helped bring in the cows from the pasture.

pasture until, without a clue as to why she had changed her mind, she would suddenly decide it was all right to go with the other cows. With a sigh of relief, I would shut the gate behind her and follow her to the barnyard. Here the cows would wait until Robert got home to do the milking. By then I would just about have supper ready to go on the table.

Old-fashioned Cottage Cheese

Go out and milk the cow. Strain 2 gallons whole milk into a big metal dishpan. Set aside until milk begins to clabber or sour slightly. Place dishpan on the back of a range or over very low heat. Warm gradually. The heat causes the curds and whey to separate. Drain curds through a colander, put curds into a clean cloth bag, hang on the clothesline, and let drain completely. Put curds in a bowl and pour sweet thick country cream over them. Mix well and serve sugared or plain and with a little salt and pepper if you like. Or go to your local grocery store and buy a carton of prepared cottage cheese of your choice. It won't taste the same, however; no one has ever duplicated the sharp, fresh taste of farm-made cottage cheese.

Cottage Cheese Salad

1 small carton cottage cheese
4 1/2 ounces prepared whipped
  topping
1 20-ounce can crushed pineapple,
  drained

1/2 cup chopped pecans
2 1/2 cups small marshmallows or
  diced large ones

Combine ingredients and chill well. Makes 8 to 10 servings.

Buttermilk Salad

2 envelopes unflavored gelatin
1/2 cup cold water
2 cups buttermilk
1 cup half-and-half

4 ounces whipped topping
1/4 cup sugar
1/2 teaspoon almond flavoring
fruits and nuts as desired

Dissolve gelatin in cold water. Heat buttermilk and stir in gelatin. When dissolved and cooled, add half-and-half. Stir in thawed whipped topping, sugar, and flavoring. Add well-drained fruits and/or nuts. Bananas are good as are candied fruits, nuts, dates, etc. Pour into mold and chill until set. Unmold on lettuce leaves. Serves 8 to 10.

Bread Pudding

2 cups milk, scalded
4 cups coarse bread pieces
1/4 cup butter or margarine, melted
1/2 cup sugar
3 eggs, slightly beaten

1/4 teaspoon salt
1 teaspoon cinnamon
1/2 cup raisins
1/2 teaspoon vanilla flavoring
1/2 teaspoon almond flavoring

Mix ingredients in a greased baking dish in the order given. Set in a pan of hot water in a 350-degree oven and bake 40 to 50 minutes or until a table knife inserted in the center comes out clean. Makes about 8 servings.

Top-of-the-Stove Bread Pudding

1 cup brown sugar, packed	2 cups milk
3 to 5 slices buttered bread, cubed	1/4 teaspoon salt
1/2 cup raisins	1/2 teaspoon vanilla flavoring
3 eggs	

Put sugar, bread cubes, and raisins in the top of a double boiler. Beat the eggs and add milk, salt, and flavoring. Pour over the sugar and bread. Have water underneath boiling and cook, covered, for about 1 hour. Do not stir (the brown sugar makes a syrup). Makes 4 or 5 servings.

Baby Cream Puffs

1 cup boiling water	1/4 teaspoon salt
1/2 cup butter or margarine	4 eggs
1 cup flour	

Combine water and butter or margarine in a pan and stir as butter or margarine melts. Add flour and salt all at once and continue to cook, stirring vigorously, until mixture is smooth and forms a ball. Remove from the fire and let cool slightly. Add eggs one at a time and beat vigorously after each addition. When all have been added and mixture is smooth and shiny, drop from a spoon on greased cookie sheet. Bake at 450 degrees for 12 minutes, then turn heat to 325 degrees and continue cooking for about 25 minutes. Cool and then slit through the center (middle of the puff should be hollow). Fill with boiled custard or whipped cream or whipped topping. Decorate with a squiggle of chocolate if desired. Makes about 2 dozen.

Boiled Custard

1/4 cup cornstarch
1/2 cup sugar
1/4 teaspoon salt
2 cups milk
2 eggs, slightly beaten

2 tablespoons butter or margarine
1 teaspoon vanilla flavoring
dates, nuts, and well-drained
    canned fruits or fresh fruits

Combine dry ingredients in heavy saucepan. Gradually beat in milk. Cook over low to moderate heat, stirring constantly, until it begins to thicken. Add a small amount of the hot mixture to slightly beaten eggs, then return eggs gradually to custard mixture. Cook 2 or 3 minutes or until mixture thickens—traditional directions say the "custard sheets from a spoon." Remove from heat and add butter and flavoring. Cool. Serve plain or fold in dates, nuts, and fruits and spoon into pretty sherbet glasses. Chill. Top with whipped cream or whipped topping and a nut or maraschino cherry. Perfect for cream puff filling. Serves 4 to 6.

Baked Custard

4 cups milk
1/4 cup sugar
1/4 teaspoon salt

1 1/2 teaspoons vanilla flavoring
4 eggs

Heat milk and sugar together to scalding. Stir to dissolve sugar. Remove from fire, add salt and flavoring. Beat eggs until yolks and whites are blended. Mix with a little of the hot milk, then gradually stir warmed eggs into milk mixture. Pour into custard cups and set in pan of hot water. Top each with a shake of nutmeg. Bake in a 350-degree oven for about 40 minutes or until a knife inserted comes out clean. Eat warm or refrigerate to eat cold. Serves about 8.

Hot Milk Cake

2 eggs
1 cup sugar
1 cup sifted flour
1/8 teaspoon salt

1 teaspoon baking powder
1 tablespoon butter
1/2 cup hot milk
1 teaspoon lemon flavoring

Beat eggs until light and lemon colored and thick. Add sugar and continue beating about 5 minutes. Fold in combined dry ingredients. Heat butter and milk together and add all at once and fold in quickly, no more than 1 minute. Add flavoring. Pour into a waxed paper–lined 8-by-8-inch square pan and bake at 350 degrees for 30 minutes. For cupcakes, bake in paper-lined cups for about 20 minutes. The cake will pull away from the side of the pan more than most cakes, but that is normal. This is excellent plain or frosted with a thin powdered sugar glaze. Makes 9 pieces.

Rice Pudding

3/4 cup uncooked rice
1 quart milk
1 to 2 cups half-and-half
3 to 4 tablespoons sugar

pinch of salt
2 tablespoons butter or margarine
1/2 teaspoon vanilla flavoring
1/2 teaspoon almond flavoring

Wash rice well and place in top of double boiler, add milk. Cover and cook over boiling water until rice is tender—about 45 minutes. Stir several times. Add remaining ingredients. Spoon into bowls and sprinkle with cinnamon. Add raisins if desired. Serves about 8.

Tapioca Pudding

3 tablespoons minute tapioca   2 cups milk
1/3 cup sugar   2 eggs
dash of salt   1 teaspoon vanilla flavoring

Combine tapioca, sugar, salt, and milk and cook in heavy pan over low heat, stirring constantly, until mixture boils well and thickens. Stir a little hot pudding, into the eggs, return eggs gradually to the pudding, and continue cooking 1 or 2 more minutes. Remove from fire and stir in flavoring. Serves 4 or 5.

7. Water

~~~~~~~~~~~~~~~~~~~~~~~~
_____

Early homesteads were situated as close to a water source as possible. The farm families used streams, ponds, or fresh springs for their livestock, for personal use, and, before the advent of ice chests and refrigerators, as places to cool food.

Many early landowners dug wells in places where they could tap into aquifers, and they drew the water up with buckets lowered on ropes. Later, well drillers came through the countryside bringing equipment to sink pipes far enough into the ground to reach those deep layers of porous rocks, sand, and gravel that were both purifiers and natural storage places for water. A pump at ground level made it possible for anyone who could move the handle up and down to receive a gush of fresh, cool water.

The earlier inhabitants of Cottonwood Farm pumped and carried into the house every drop of water they used for drinking, food preparation, laundry, cleaning, and baths. Several years before our arrival, Cottonwood Farm's owner had installed a sink in the kitchen and piped water from the backyard well to an underground reservoir or cistern on the hill behind the barn. A windmill located over the well pumped water up the hill to the cistern. Gravity carried the water from there to the kitchen sink and into the animal stock tanks in the barn-

Windmills were among the most energy-efficient machines on a farm. Dempster Industries, Inc.

Robert could put this stock tank on a low wagon bed and haul water out to the animals in fields that had no other water source. When it was empty, it was a play space for Bob (left) and cousin Bill Barnard (right).

yards and feedlots. Robert kept the water in the tanks from freezing in the winter by immersing in each one a Cowboy brand cast-iron stove that burned cobs, wood scraps, or coal so that the cows, pigs, and sheep would have water to drink during the coldest months.

As the only water source in the house, our kitchen sink served many purposes: rinsing clothes, brushing teeth, shampooing hair, and washing dishes, and for Robert's shaving. When they were small, the children could fit into the sink for their baths, but Robert and I certainly could not. Most of the time we made do by taking sponge baths, but sometimes on warm summer days, Robert would put our large metal laundry tubs under the windmill and pump them full of water. By late afternoon, the sun would have warmed the water for our open-air baths.

With no bathroom in the house, our toilet, or "necessity," as some people called the outhouse, was reached by going out the back door,

Outdoor toilets were still used in the 1940s and 1950s near schools, churches, and farmhouses that did not have plumbing. Shenandoah Evening Sentinel photo.

down the porch steps, around the house, and up a short path. Warm weather trips could be downright pleasant. The little building was secluded from the road and out of sight of anyone in the house. A person sitting on one of the two holes could leave the door open and watch the clouds moving across the sky and the branches of the cottonwood trees blowing in the breeze. Lingering was not on anyone's mind in the winter, however, when the temperature dropped and the cold winds blew.

Some farmers provisioned their outhouses with old Sears and Montgomery Ward catalogs. These did provide inexpensive reading and wiping material, but I never succumbed to that form of frugality. Each week my grocery list included at least one package of store-bought toilet paper. Small as our income was, I preferred to economize in other ways.

During exceptionally blustery weather or when someone was ill, I used the time-honored pioneer method of putting a toilet receptacle under each bed or in the back storage room. These utilitarian objects were called by various names—"thunder mugs," "chamber pots," "slop jars." They were as unpleasant to care for as the names imply.

I often looked out the kitchen window at the windmill and thought that it really was strong enough and the water supply sufficient to provide water for a bathroom in the house, and I dreamed of the day it would become a reality. But this period in Middle America was still a time when landowners considered updating the plumbing in the houses of the hired hands or renters a luxury, not a necessity, and so I dreamed on.

Sometimes when I walked along the banks of Mill Creek I dreamed as well of the time when its water was clear and unpolluted. The soft soils of the southwest Iowa hills are prone to severe erosion. Before current practices of terracing and conservation tillage, plowing the fields loosened the rich earth, and the spring rains swept the topsoil down into rivers and creeks. The same rains that turned the farmyards and lanes into quagmires of mud also drained off the land, adding animal wastes to the streams. Later in the century, farmers gained the knowledge, equipment, and government cost-sharing programs to reduce the erosion and pollution, but during our years on the farm we and our neighbors just did the best we knew how.

Farm families often used the deep ravines in their land as places to deposit trash. Castoffs that could not be burned had to go somewhere, so all farmers had a place where they threw battered kitchen utensils, worn-out appliances, rusting farm machinery, and even old cars. Some farmers tossed dead animals into gullies, reasoning that silt would eventually cover the carcasses. A number of the landowners thought that any fill would stop erosion in the ravines, and some of the larger discarded items did help hold the soil in place.

Towns sometimes maintained a dump where people could dispose of their trash. Those who were less thoughtful just drove into the country and tossed bags of refuse over the bridges into the creeks or into ditches along the roadside. Wherever the refuse was discarded, the summer rains and the runoff from the winter snows flowed through it and added more pollution to the streams.

Because of its contamination, Robert declared Mill Creek off limits for our family play except in the winter when it was frozen over. Fortunately, Cottonwood Farm had two lovely, clear, spring-fed brooks for warm weather recreation. We held campfires and wiener roasts on their banks, took walks in the bordering grasses, enjoyed the wildflowers that grew in the moist soil, and waded in their cool, clean waters.

In the spring the children liked to catch tadpoles in the brooks. They put some of the funny wigglers into glass jars filled with water and placed them on the back porch to watch as the tadpoles absorbed their tails and grew miniature legs. Eventually, the youngsters carried the jars back to the streams and turned the diminutive amphibians loose. Later, on summer evenings, when we heard the croaking call of frogs, we were certain they were the same creatures that had spent time evolving on our back porch.

The well water served many purposes for our family, but none I relished more than when I made it into tea. When the minister and his wife came to call in the afternoon I made tea. When I was tired and just needed to stop for a brief respite I made a cup. When Robert came into the house for a mid-afternoon pause in whatever work he was doing, I brewed a pot. When I had time, I made scones or cinnamon sticks and arranged a tea party with the children. I filled each child's cup half full of milk and then poured in strong, hot tea—"cambric tea" Grandma Corrie had called the drink when she prepared it for me when I was small.

Our favorite place to drink tea during warm weather was under one

We celebrated Dulcie Jean's third birthday with a tea party in the yard.

of the big cottonwood trees in the backyard. I set up the card table and chairs and put out the food. As we drank our tea and nibbled on our sweets, we watched for butterflies and birds, looked across the fields toward Mill Creek, and listened to the musical sounds made by the windmill as its big wheel turned gently in the breeze.

Cinnamon Toast Sticks

Use a loaf of unsliced bread. Cut the long way into 1-inch slices. Cut each slice into 1-inch strips. Roll each bread stick in melted butter or margarine. Combine 1/3 cup sugar with 1 teaspoon cinnamon and roll buttered bread sticks in this mixture. Place bread sticks on cookie sheet and bake in a 375-degree oven until toasted. Or just use slices of buttered bread, sprinkle with cinnamon mixture, toast in oven, and cut the resulting cinnamon toast into strips and serve. Make as many as you want.

Cinnamon Dip (Sauce)

2 tablespoons flour
2 tablespoons brown sugar, packed
1/2 teaspoon cinnamon

1 cup water
1 tablespoon butter or margarine
1/2 teaspoon vanilla flavoring

Combine flour, brown sugar, cinnamon, and water in a saucepan. Cook, stirring, until thick. Stir in butter and flavoring and serve hot over gingerbread or leftover cake. Why this recipe is called Cinnamon Dip is unknown to me. It is a simple sauce that my mother served over any cake which had been around for a day or two and needed perking up.

Tea Party Scones

2 cups flour
2 teaspoons baking powder
1 tablespoon sugar
6 tablespoons butter, diced

1/2 cup currants or raisins
  (optional)
2 large eggs, well beaten
1/2 cup milk, cream, or half-and-
  half

Sift dry ingredients into bowl. Add butter and work into dry ingredients with fingertips until mixture resembles coarse cornmeal. Toss in currants or raisins. Make a well in dry ingredients and add well-beaten eggs. Gradually add milk (or cream or half-and-half) and stir until mixture is moistened and dough holds together. Knead about 10 times in the bowl and turn out on lightly floured breadboard. Cut in half and make each half into a ball. Pat flat in greased, round pie pans. Brush tops with a little milk or cream and sprinkle lightly with sugar. Bake at

425 degrees for about 12 to 15 minutes or until lightly browned. These can be made ahead and then reheated in oven or microwave. They also freeze well to bring out later and heat. Individual scones can be made by cutting the dough with a round cookie cutter. Bake on a greased cookie sheet at 425 degrees for 8 to 10 minutes or until brown. Makes about 10.

Old-fashioned Shortcake

4 cups flour
4 teaspoons baking powder
2/3 cup sugar
1/4 teaspoon salt

1/2 cup butter or margarine
1 1/2 cups milk
2 eggs, beaten

Sift dry ingredients together. Cut in butter or margarine until mixture resembles fine crumbs. Combine milk and eggs and stir in just enough to moisten ingredients. Pat into three greased 9-inch round pans or pie pans and bake at 425 degrees for about 20 minutes or until lightly browned. Cut into wedges, split, and serve with sweetened fruit. Great with cream or whipped cream. These can also be cut into circles. Bake on greased cookie sheet for about 15 minutes or until lightly browned. Makes 10 to 12 servings.

Teatime Sponge Drops

1 1/2 cups flour
1/8 teaspoon salt
3 egg yolks
1/2 cup sugar

1 tablespoon cold water
1/2 teaspoon lemon flavoring
1/2 teaspoon grated lemon rind
3 egg whites

Sift flour and salt together. Beat egg yolks until thick and lemon colored. Continue beating and gradually add sugar, water, flavoring, lemon rind, and the flour mixture and continue beating until batter is stiff. Beat egg whites until soft peaks form and gently fold into batter. Drop batter from a teaspoon on greased and floured cookie sheet. Bake at 350 degrees for 8 to 10 minutes or until light brown around the edges. Make a powdered sugar icing with lemon flavoring or lemon juice and use as a filling between cookies to make little dainty teatime sandwich cookies. Makes 1 1/2 dozen.

Marshmallow Bars

CRUST

3/4 cup margarine
1/3 cup brown sugar, packed
1 1/4 cups flour

Combine ingredients and press into a greased 9-by-13-inch baking pan. Bake at 325 degrees for 20 minutes. Cool.

TOPPING

2 envelopes unflavored gelatin
1/2 cup cold water
2 cups sugar
1/4 cup maraschino cherry juice
pinch of salt
1 1/2 teaspoons vanilla flavoring

1/4 cup water
1/2 cup nuts
1/2 cup drained chopped
  maraschino cherries
coconut (optional)

Dissolve gelatin in 1/2 cup cold water. Combine sugar, cherry juice, salt, flavoring, and remaining 1/4 cup water. Bring to a boil and boil for 2 minutes. Remove from heat and gradually stir in gelatin mixture and beat with mixer at high speed until the consistency of divinity. Fold in nuts and well-drained cherries. Spoon over baked and cooled crust and sprinkle coconut on top. Cut into squares. For a variation, put individual vanilla wafers in the bottoms of muffin tins and spoon the topping mixture over each cookie. Let set. (Notice that no marsh-mallows are included in this recipe. The topping is a marshmallow-type mixture.) Makes about a dozen bars.

Petticoat Tails

2 cups butter, softened
1 cup sifted powdered sugar
1 teaspoon almond or vanilla
    flavoring

3 cups sifted flour
3/4 cup cornstarch
dash of salt

Combine ingredients and mix well with hands. Shape into a ball. Wrap in waxed paper and chill until firm. Pat dough about 3/4 inch thick in ungreased pie pans. Prick with a fork and bake at 375 degrees for about 5 minutes, then lower the temperature to 325 degrees and continue cooking about 30 minutes or until golden on top but not brown. Cut into wedges, which makes these into "petticoat tails." These keep very well in a tightly covered container. Makes about 75.

Gingerbread

2 eggs, beaten
1 cup brown sugar, packed
3/4 cup butter or margarine, melted
3/4 cup molasses
1 cup buttermilk
1 teaspoon vanilla flavoring

3 cups flour
1 teaspoon baking soda
1/4 teaspoon salt
1 teaspoon ginger
1 teaspoon cinnamon

Beat eggs, sugar, butter or margarine, and molasses together, stir in buttermilk and flavoring. Sift dry ingredients together and add to creamed mixture. Beat until blended. Pour into a buttered 9-by-13-inch pan. Bake 30 minutes or until gingerbread tests done. Makes about 15 pieces.

Local people in southwest Iowa fished in the rivers and farm ponds. Catfish, bullheads, and carp abounded in the years when the waters were reasonably clear. When fresh fish weren't available, the housewives used canned fish to vary their menus.

Country Fried Catfish

1 cup flour

1 cup cornmeal

salt to taste

peanut oil

Rinse catfish. Pat lightly with a paper towel. Combine dry ingredients and coat fish with mixture. Heat peanut oil until a bread cube dropped in sizzles. Fry fish, turning to brown on both sides. Delicious served with Hush Puppies.

Hush Puppies

1 1/2 cups cornmeal

1 1/2 cups flour

2 teaspoons baking powder

1/2 teaspoon salt

dash of pepper

1 egg

1 cup milk

1 small onion, grated

Mix together well and drop from a teaspoon (small amount) in fat in which fish has been fried or in hot shortening. Flip over once and cook about 3 minutes or until brown. Makes about 2 dozen.

Salmon Loaf

1 14 3/4-ounce can salmon

1/2 cup salmon liquid and milk

1 cup saltine cracker crumbs

2 tablespoons lemon juice

2 tablespoons diced onion

1 egg

salt and pepper to taste

Strain liquid from salmon into measuring cup and add enough milk to make 1/2 cup. Remove skin and bones from drained salmon and discard. Flake salmon into bowl. Combine ingredients. Put into greased bread loaf pan and bake at 350 degrees for 30 minutes or until set. Makes 6 to 8 servings.

Salmon Patties

Use recipe for Salmon Loaf but eliminate liquid. Shape into patties and fry in butter, margarine, or oil, or spray skillet with a fat-free coating and fry with fewer calories. Excellent served with fried or baked potatoes, a green salad, cooked carrots, and canned or fresh peaches. Makes about 6 patties.

Jellied Salmon

2 envelopes unflavored gelatin
1 cup cold water
2 hard-cooked eggs, sliced
2/3 cup lemon juice
2 14 3/4-ounce cans salmon

1 1/2 cups mayonnaise
2 cups diced celery
1/2 cup diced sweet green pepper
salt to taste

Soften gelatin in cold water in top of double boiler. Dissolve by placing over hot water. Arrange egg slices in bottom of oiled bread pan. Pour a thin layer of melted gelatin over eggs and chill in refrigerator until set. Remove bones and skin from salmon and drain off liquid. Combine with other ingredients including remaining gelatin and spoon over egg layer. Chill until firm. Turn out on lettuce leaves and garnish with sliced hard-cooked eggs and tomatoes. Can substitute 4 7-ounce cans of tuna fish for the salmon. A fine buffet dish. Serves 12 or more.

Baked Fish

2 teaspoons salt   2 pounds fish or fish fillets
1 cup milk   1 cup crushed corn flakes

Dissolve salt in milk. Dip fish into the milk and then into crushed corn flakes. Bake on a greased cookie sheet in a hot oven—about 450 degrees—until nicely browned, about 20 minutes depending on size of the fish. Makes about 4 servings.

8. Laundry

~~~~~~~~~~~~~~~~~~~~~~~~~~~~
_____

As surely as the sun came up in the east and went down in the west, farm women of the 1940s and 1950s washed clothes on Monday and ironed on Tuesday. Only illness or death would keep those housewives from their appointed schedules. No one could tell me why Monday was washday and Tuesday was for ironing, but I wasn't about to vary from a routine everyone kept.

I learned early on that midwesterners pronounce the word *wash* with an extra consonant—"warsh." Soon after our move to the farm I also realized that doing my "warsh" on Monday reflected on my efficiency. The earlier I could get the clothes out on the line, and the whiter and cleaner they looked, the brighter my reputation as a good wife and homemaker. My real purpose in getting the washing out early was not to impress the neighbors, however. I just wanted to get as much of it completed as possible before the children got out of bed.

Our square-tub Maytag washing machine with an attached wringer and two rinse tubs stood near the cream separator on the back porch. I began the laundry by fastening a hose to the kitchen sink and running it out the back door and into the washing machine tub to fill it with hot water. I did the same with the first rinse tub and then filled the second with cold water.

I added powdered laundry soap and water softener to the water in the washing machine and put a few drops of Mrs. Stewart's Liquid Bluing in the cold water for the last rinse. Bluing was a product that promised to "offset any yellowish tinge in white fabrics and make them snow-white." The directions on the bottle assured me that Mrs. Stewart's would "make the water sky blue."

The Maytag's electric-powered agitator churned the clothes through the suds, but that was all it did—no automatic rinse-and-spin cycle in this machine. To get the soap and water out of the clothing, I used a smooth broomstick with the broom cut off to lift each piece out of the hot water and up to a wringer mounted above the washer, then pushed the washed clothing close to the rollers which caught the fabric and pulled it through to squeeze out the soapy water. The damp garments plopped into the first rinse tub. Still wielding the stick, I sloshed everything up and down in the hot rinse. We believed then that only very hot wash water would get the clothes really clean, especially the white things, so using the stick kept my hands from being scalded. After the first rinse, I ran everything through the wringer again, swished the clothes in the cold water, then put them through the rollers a final time and let them drop into a wicker basket on the floor.

Since I used the wash and rinse water over and over again, I first washed the bed sheets (four to eight per wash), towels, dish cloths, and the good Sunday shirts, then moved on to the children's clothes, the colored things, and finally Robert's work clothes. By then the wash water would be cloudy and the rinse water lukewarm, but even Robert's last pair of overalls came out surprisingly clean.

While I was busy on the porch sloshing and wringing, I prepared the starch. I measured out half a cup of dry white chunks of Niagara or Argo starch—which they decreed would "give a beauty bath to all your starchables"—added two quarts of water, and left the mixture to simmer until it was clear and thick. After I had thinned it with a little cold water, I dipped the washed cotton garments into the starch so that they would iron smoothly and stay clean through several wearings. The shirts needed the heaviest starching, so I dipped them first, then did the aprons, dresses, little girl pinafores, and little boy shirts and pants.

While it was true that this 1946 washer made washdays much easier, I found that even as I used my similar square-tub Maytag it was an exaggeration to say doing the laundry was "no work." Maytag Company.

I twisted each garment by hand to wring out the excess starch. Instant starch came on the market in the early 1950s, but it was more expensive, so I continued to use the cooked method during the years we lived on the farm.

The wicker basket was heavy by the time I carried the soggy laundry

I enjoyed hanging up clothes in the warm months of the year.
Winter, however, was a different matter.

outside to the clothesline. I wiped the dust off the line with a damp cloth, then used wooden clothespins to fasten everything to the heavy wires. Some of the women I knew carefully hung each part of their laundry certain ways. One might put the two open ends of a sheet together and fasten this section of the sheet to the clothesline. Another might toss the sheet over the line, even up the bottom edges, and then push the clothespins over the wire to hold it tight. Each housewife felt that her way was preferable to all others, so I tried them all and never noticed any difference in the outcome. Left long enough in the sun and wind, my laundry always got dry, and it always had a delightful sweet scent of the outdoors that lingered long after I brought the clothing back into the house.

Despite the hours and the effort, I didn't mind doing the laundry in the summer when warm breezes blew in through the screen-covered walls of the porch. Doing the wash in the winter was quite another matter. Even though Robert covered the screens with weather-glass to keep out the chilling wind, the unheated porch was still very cold. One Monday, a winter wind blew off the south wall of the porch. Robert had gone to help one of the neighbors get machinery ready for spring planting, so I had to cope alone as best I could with cranky kids, an icy porch, and a huge laundry.

Robert repaired the porch by the following Monday, but even sheltered from the wind I often ran the washing machine in temperatures below freezing, and I still hung the laundry outdoors most of the time. The clothes on the line froze into weird, grotesque shapes, especially Robert's long underwear, the legs and arms twisted about like those of icicle scarecrows. When the clothesline was full, I laid the last items—usually Robert's overalls—over the yard fence.

I brought the frozen laundry inside as soon as I thought it was dry (I never did figure out how fabric could freeze dry), and then the real fun began. I set the stiff overalls and underwear and towels near the kitchen stove and laughed as they thawed and slowly crumpled on the floor like melting snowmen.

If laundry day brought rain or snow, I abandoned the clothesline and hung the clothes on racks near the heating stove in the living room. The wet laundry helped moisturize the winter-dry air in the house. It also steamed up the windows, and the children used their fingers to draw pictures on the foggy glass. On the coldest days, when frost painted the windows with sparkling fronds like a strange fairy forest, we all enjoyed using metal thimbles or cookie cutters to press designs into the icy panes.

After the last of the washing was done in the winter, Robert carried the buckets of water out to the hog lot and emptied them into a drainage ditch. On summer Mondays, I poured the rinse water on the plants growing in the garden and on the flower beds near the house. Then I scrubbed the porch floor with the soapy wash water.

The laundry work did not stop when the clothes were dry and I had taken them off the lines and yard fence, folded them into the basket, and carried them into the house. The next step was to sprinkle everything made of cotton—shirts, dresses, pillow cases, and the like—with water from a pop bottle with a metal salt-shaker-like lid stuck into it. I rolled up the dampened items and tucked them into a wicker basket, then covered them with a heavy bath towel. The fabric gradually absorbed the moisture, making it ready for ironing by the following morning.

Like everyone else, I did my ironing on Tuesdays. In the winter I would set the ironing board near the kitchen window, and in the summer I put it on the back porch. My electric iron was a far cry from the heavy "sad irons" heated on the coal ranges by my mother's generation, but it was still a long way from the steam irons that came later and put an end to the sprinkling and dampening chores. I found it pleasant to watch the iron glide over the surface of the material as I made the wrinkles disappear and a smooth, fresh surface take their place. I often put my favorite records on the phonograph or encouraged the children to put their selections on to keep us company with music and stories. Ironing day was also a perfect time for dreaming. My body might be confined to the chores before me, but my mind never stayed captive for long.

Most country women prepared simple meals on washing and ironing days, usually made with ingredients that could simmer away untended on the stove or could be thrown together quickly. Succulent navy bean soup cooked with a ham bone was our favorite, especially when I baked a pan of corn bread to serve with it. Other special delights gleaned from the laundry day menus of my mother, sister, and neighbors included croquettes, shepherd's pie, and hash made from leftover roast.

Soup Beans and Ham

2 cups white or Great Northern
    beans
water to cover
1 teaspoon baking soda
1 large onion

1 large cured ham bone or ham
    shank (or pieces of cured sliced
    ham)
2 carrots, shredded
1 potato, diced

Look over beans and remove any that are black or unsightly. Wash good beans well. Place in a heavy 4-quart saucepan or pressure pan. Cover with water and soak for 1 hour. Add 1 teaspoon baking soda and bring to a boil uncovered. This foams up, so keep heat moderate to low. Boil 15 minutes, then drain and rinse. This step helps cut much of the acid from the beans. Cover with fresh warm water, add onion and ham, and cook until beans are almost tender. Add carrots and potato and continue cooking until done. Taste and add seasonings as needed. I usually cook the beans in my pressure pan at 10 pounds for 20 minutes. Then I bring the pressure down under cold running water, open the lid and add the carrots and potato, and bring the pressure back to 10 pounds. Cook 3 more minutes and the soup is done. Serve with corn bread. Serves at least 6.

Sweet Milk Corn Bread

1 cup white flour
1 cup yellow cornmeal
4 teaspoons baking powder
1/2 teaspoon salt

1/2 cup sugar
2 eggs
1 cup milk
3 tablespoons melted butter

Put dry ingredients into a bowl. Beat eggs and stir in along with the milk and melted butter. Spoon into a well-greased 8-by-8-inch pan and bake in a 400-degree oven for 20 minutes or until brown. Makes 9 squares.

Beef and Noodle Soup

1 pound stew meat
1 soup bone (optional)
1/4 cup flour
2 teaspoons salt

1 teaspoon sweet marjoram
1 quart of water
3 medium potatoes, diced
1 cup uncooked egg noodles

Combine flour and seasonings, coat meat and soup bone with this mixture and brown in a little shortening. Add water and simmer until meat is tender, 1 hour or so. Remove meat from bone, cut into bite-sized pieces, and return to broth. Add potatoes and noodles to boiling broth and continue cooking until tender. Serve hot. Homemade noodles are marvelous in this soup, but so are the wide store-bought noodles broken into small squares. Serves 6 to 8.

Shepherd's Pie

1 medium onion, diced
1 pound ground beef (or leftover
  roast)
salt and pepper to taste
2 cups cooked green beans, drained

1 10 3/4-ounce can tomato soup
2 to 3 cups mashed potatoes
1 egg, beaten
1/2 cup grated cheese

Sauté onion in a little shortening until golden. Add meat and seasonings. Brown. Add beans and soup and spoon into 1 1/2 quart greased casserole. Combine mashed potatoes and egg with seasonings to taste. Spoon mounds of the potatoes over top of meat mixture. Sprinkle cheese over top and bake at 350 degrees for 30 minutes. Leftover beef roast is good in this dish. Grind or chop meat into bite-sized pieces and continue as directed. Serves 6.

Goulash

1 medium onion, minced
1 clove garlic, minced
1 tablespoon butter
1 pound ground beef

2 cups canned or fresh tomatoes
1 to 2 cups cooked macaroni or rice
salt and pepper to taste

Brown onion and garlic in butter, add ground beef and brown lightly. Stir in tomatoes and macaroni or rice. Add seasonings to taste. Cook and stir until cooked through or bake in a 300-degree oven for 1 hour. Serves 6 to 8.

Potato Soup

3 cups diced raw potatoes
1 carrot, shredded
1/4 cup chopped onion
1 to 2 cups water

2 cups milk
salt and pepper to taste
2 tablespoons butter or margarine
1 tablespoon flour

Put potatoes, carrot, onion, and water in a kettle. Cover and simmer until tender. Do not drain. Add milk, seasonings, and butter or margarine. Mix flour with a little cold milk and stir in. Continue simmering, stirring occasionally, until mixture thickens slightly. Serve in bowls with crumbled bacon and a little butter or margarine spooned on top. Serves 4 or 5.

Old-fashioned Cream of Corn Soup

6 ears sweet corn (or 2 cups frozen
    or canned)
3/4 cup grated onion
4 cups milk
3 tablespoons flour

3 tablespoons butter
1/2 cup half-and-half or milk
    (optional)
salt and pepper to taste

Cut corn from cob (or use frozen or canned). Combine with onion and milk. Heat slowly to boiling. Cream flour and butter together and half-and-half or milk and stir with fork until creamy consistency. Add to soup and stir, cooking until thick. Season. Serve as is or mixture can be strained for a creamy corn soup. Makes 6 cups.

Quick-and-Easy Hash

2 cups chopped cooked meat
2 cups chopped onion
2 cups diced cooked potatoes

1 cup broth or gravy
salt and pepper

Brown meat, onion, and potatoes in a little shortening or oil in a skillet. Add broth or gravy and simmer, covered, until heated through. Season to taste. Add a little more liquid if it gets too dry. This is a simple, tasty dish made with leftover pork or beef roast.

9. Stoves

Life in many farm homes centered in good part around the kitchen. Up until World War II, most kitchens were dominated by coal- and wood-burning cooking ranges. The cookstove was usually a large, black, cast-iron unit decorated with enamel trim on the doors of the baking oven and the warming ovens. The warming ovens looked like a hood lifting above the top of the cooking surface. A farm wife could put food on the shelves inside and keep it warm. The warming ovens were also a dry, convenient place for her to store the spices she used to season her recipes.

My range seemed to be constantly in need of polish. I would take a bottle of stove black and with a rag rub the cool iron surfaces with what looked like liquid shoe polish. The shiny finish burned off with the next hot fire, but at least for a time the stove looked fresh and clean, and the stove black helped keep the iron from rusting. At first I tried to polish our range once a week, but as time went on, I made the effort only when company was coming.

The stove's "lifter" was a metal handle shaped to fit into a slot in each round lid covering the firebox. I lifted those lids when I wanted to add more fuel. When I wanted water in a kettle to boil faster, I often took

We used a Monarch coal/cob/wood cooking range when we moved to the farm. The lifter for the stove lids is near the tea kettle (left), the reservoir filled with rainwater is on the right, and on top is a pan with which we dipped out the warm water. *Shenandoah Evening Sentinel* photo.

off one of the lids and set the kettle right over the flames. The fire speeded the cooking, but it also blackened the bottom of the kettle.

I especially appreciated the reservoir at one end of the stove, which the heat from the fire kept warm. Robert filled the reservoir with "soft" rainwater from the barrel under the house eaves. We preferred the soft water for washing dishes, hair, hands, and faces, since the soap dissolved in it easily. In contrast, groundwater picks up the minerals from the soil, and the minerals make that water "hard."

When I was first learning to use the range, everything I baked in the oven either burned because I had the fire blazing too high or was underdone because I had let the fire burn too low. Eventually, I mastered the art of feeding a fire just enough fuel for any baking project. During the cold months when the range was going most of the time to help heat the house, I could leave the coffeepot on the stove and keep it hot all day. I also learned to put on a kettle of stew, soup beans, or beef stock to simmer through the afternoon as the foundation for a hearty evening meal.

Besides cooking our food, the kitchen range had other important purposes on the farm. I sometimes folded pieces of old clean blankets over a chair by the oven door. When they were warm, Robert took them to the farrowing house or lambing shed to wrap around shivering, wet, newborn animals. If the electricity went out in the brooder house, I would bring in a box of peeping baby chicks and place it behind the stove to keep them warm until the heat lamp functioned again. Robert often carried squealing baby pigs and bleating lambs into the kitchen to get them dry and warm, then returned them to their mothers.

On stormy days I frequently hung wet laundry on a rack in front of the open oven door, and I would put wet mittens and overshoes on the door to dry. I've even heard stories of country folks keeping a newborn baby warm by swaddling the infant in blankets and letting the baby sleep on the open oven door—a primitive form of incubator.

For stove fuel, Robert cut fallen limbs from the cottonwood trees into kindling the proper size for the stove box. He stored the corncobs left from the previous autumn harvest in a wooden shed near the garage and, because they burn quickly, used them for early morning fires to warm the house. Each night before bedtime he crumpled up newspapers and put them into the cold firebox of the kitchen range, then put a layer of kerosene-soaked cobs on top. Before daylight, he would get out of bed and light the paper with a match. When the fire was blazing, he would put in sticks of wood and a few pieces of coal.

In addition to the kitchen range, many rural homes had heating stoves in the living room. Our first such stove was a Warm Morning, a large stove which took up a considerable amount of space in our small room. It was blocky in shape with a fire brick interior and a cream-colored enamel exterior. It had a glass window in the door through which we could see the glow of the burning coal and wood. A black pipe carried away the smoke to a chimney in the wall that rose above the roof of the house. A box behind the stove held wood, but we kept the coal bucket on the back porch, carrying it into the living room only long enough to add fuel to the fire, which helped keep some of the coal dust out of the living room.

Robert moved the Warm Morning stove out to a shed during the warm months when we didn't need the heat, and I enjoyed having the extra space in the small living room. But the moment a chill autumn wind blew down into Mill Creek Valley, he brought the stove back inside to add its warmth to our drafty house for at least six months of the year.

On frosty winter mornings, I liked to lie snug and drowsy in bed at dawn and listen to the sounds Robert made as he started the fires. I could hear him moving the grates back and forth so the ashes in the stoves would fall into the trays underneath. I could hear him clang the lids of the range and the door of the Warm Morning stove as he added fuel to the fires. Gradually the heat radiated throughout the house. When I felt the air grow warm in the bedroom, I knew it was time for me to get up.

Neither of those stoves lasted through our years at Cottonwood Farm. Eventually the Warm Morning stove gave way to an oil-burning heater, still set in the corner of the living room with a black stove pipe disappearing into the wall. It was a decided improvement over the

Our neighbors, Ed and Anna Nelson, had an oil heating stove
much like ours. Their two granddaughters, Gayle Nelson and
Delona Walters, are getting warm in front of the stove.
Nora Nelson photo.

earlier stove, however, for we no longer needed to walk through the
house carrying wood and coal. The heat was more constant, too, but I
did miss seeing the cheerful glow of the fire that used to blaze behind
the glass window of the Warm Morning stove.

By the 1950s, most of our neighbors had replaced wood and coal
stoves and ranges with those that burned oil or gas. When we finally
exchanged our old kitchen range for a clean gas cookstove, we felt we

had truly achieved a higher standard of living. The new kitchen stove drew propane from tanks outside the porch door. When we had an empty tank, we called a serviceperson from town who would bring us a replacement.

With the gas cookstove I had a constant, clean source of heat and a consistent oven temperature. I also found it much easier to keep the house cool in the summer and to keep it free from coal and wood dust all during the year. It had been a challenging experience to cook on a wood/coal-burning range and bake in its oven. I didn't miss it very much, but once in a while I would have liked that iron stove top to keep a pot of coffee hot or to slow cook a kettle of beans. Most of all, I missed the old stove when I baked bread. Of all the foods I prepared with that kitchen range, bread was my favorite.

Seven-Grain Cereal Bread

1/2 cup seven-grain cereal
1 cup water
1/3 cup butter or margarine
1/4 cup honey
1 cup water
2 teaspoons salt
2 packages yeast

1/4 cup lukewarm water
1 teaspoon sugar
5 to 6 cups unbleached flour
2 eggs
1 egg yolk
1 tablespoon water

In a small saucepan combine cereal and 1 cup water. Cook, stirring occasionally, for about 10 minutes or until tender, just like cooked oatmeal. Add more water if needed. Stir in the butter or margarine, honey, another cup water, and salt. Set aside to cool. Dissolve yeast in 1/4 cup of lukewarm water and add 1 teaspoon sugar. Put 2 cups of flour in large mixing bowl, stir in the cooled cereal mixture and the yeast mixture. Add the 2 eggs. Beat with an electric mixer for 3 minutes, starting on low and increasing to high speed. Remove mixer and stir in enough additional flour to make a soft dough. Turn out on floured breadboard and knead until smooth and elastic (dough has a springy feel)—at least 5 minutes. Shape into a ball and place in greased bowl, turn once to grease all sides. Cover and let rise in a warm, draft-free place until double. Punch down, turn out on floured breadboard, and divide into two portions. Cover with a towel or waxed paper and let dough rest 10 minutes. Knead each portion, shape into loaves, and place in greased 4-by-8-inch loaf pans. Cover and let rise until double. Combine the egg yolk with 1 tablespoon water to form an "egg wash." Brush this gently over the top of the loaves. Sprinkle with sesame or poppy seeds if desired. Bake at 375 degrees for 30 to 35 minutes or until golden brown on top and the loaves make a hollow sound when thumped. Other mixtures besides the seven-grain cereal can be used for this bread, such as steel cut oats, cracked wheat, bulgur wheat, finely chopped or ground nuts, or seeds. Part white flour and part whole wheat flour is another fine variation. Makes 2 loaves.

Plain Bread

2 packages yeast
4 1/2 cups lukewarm water
6 tablespoons sugar

1 tablespoon salt
1/4 cup shortening
12 cups flour (about)

Dissolve yeast in 1/2 cup lukewarm water. Add remaining water to mixture along with sugar, salt, and shortening. Add enough flour until dough forms a ball. Turn out on floured breadboard and knead until smooth and elastic (dough has a springy feel). Place in greased bowl, turning to grease all sides, cover, and let rise until double. Punch down and let rise again until almost double. Turn out on floured breadboard and cut into four portions. Let dough rest about 10 minutes. Knead each portion and put in greased bread pan, cut-side down. Let rise until double and bake at 375 degrees for 40 minutes or until brown and loaves make a hollow sound when thumped. Remove bread from pan and cool on rack to keep bottom from "sweating." Coat crust with butter if a tender crust is desired. Fresh, hot, homemade bread is a terrific treat, but if some of the loaves are left at the end of the day they are baked, wrap in plastic or foil and store in freezer until needed. Makes 4 loaves.

Oatmeal Bread

1 cup honey

2 teaspoons salt

1/4 cup margarine

1 cup rolled oats

1 cup dry powdered milk

1 1/2 cups boiling water

2 packages yeast

1/2 cup water

8 or 9 cups flour

Combine honey, salt, margarine, rolled oats, and dried milk. Add boiling water and mix well. Let cool to lukewarm. Add yeast to 1/2 cup warm water. When bubbly, stir into first cooled mixture. Gradually beat in flour. When you can shape dough into a ball, knead for 8 to 10 minutes on floured breadboard. Place in large greased bowl and cover with clean tea towel or plastic wrap. Let rise in a draft-free location until double. Knead down and shape into three loaves. Place in greased loaf pans, cover, and let rise until almost double. Bake at 300 degrees for 50 minutes or until loaves are brown and make a hollow sound when thumped. Makes 3 loaves.

Favorite Rolls

1 cup milk, scalded

1/4 cup shortening

1/4 cup sugar

1 teaspoon salt

1 package yeast

1/4 cup lukewarm water

1 teaspoon sugar

1 egg, beaten

3 1/2 cups flour

Scald milk. Remove from fire and add shortening, 1/4 cup sugar, and salt, stir to dissolve, then cool to lukewarm. While this is cooling, combine yeast, lukewarm water, and 1 teaspoon sugar. Let dissolve and bubble for 5 minutes. Add dissolved yeast to cooled milk mixture. Gradually beat in egg and enough flour to make a soft dough. Turn out on floured breadboard. Work in only as much flour as needed, no more; the less flour used, the lighter the rolls. Knead lightly for 3 to 4 minutes. It becomes smooth and elastic (dough has a springy feel). Place dough in greased bowl, turning once to coat all sides. Cover with clean tea towel and let rise in a draft-free place until double (about 2 hours). Punch down and knead on lightly floured board for about 5 minutes. Shape into rolls and place on greased cookie sheet or baking pan. Cover with tea towel and let rise in a warm, draft-free location until double. Bake at 375 degrees for about 20 minutes or until golden brown on top. Turn out on wire cooling rack. If you like a crusty roll, leave as is. If you want a soft crust, brush rolls with butter or margarine when removed from the oven. This is a fine yeast bread for beginners, but it is equally good for experienced cooks. Makes 2 dozen.

Cinnamon Rolls with Honey Topping

Make up Favorite Rolls. While the dough is rising for the first time, make up Honey Topping.

HONEY TOPPING

1/3 cup honey
1/2 cup brown sugar, packed

1/4 cup butter or margarine
dash of salt

Combine ingredients in saucepan and cook on moderate heat, stirring constantly, until a soft ball forms when tested in cold water (or 235 degrees on a candy thermometer). Remove from fire immediately and pour into well-buttered 9-by-13-inch baking pan. Sprinkle with chopped pecans if desired. Cool to lukewarm. After first rising, knead the dough down, divide it into two portions, roll each into a rectangle, and spread with a light coating of softened butter or margarine. Sprinkle with either white or brown sugar and cinnamon, as much as desired. Roll up like a jelly roll and slice. Lay cut-side down on top of syrup mixture. Cover and let rolls rise until double. Bake at 400 degrees about 20 minutes or until nicely brown. Turn out while hot with topping on the top. Do not cool in the pan or the syrup mixture will stick to pan.

Superb Orange Rolls

1 1/4 cups milk, scalded
1/2 cup butter or margarine
1/3 cup sugar
1/2 teaspoon salt
1 package yeast
1 teaspoon sugar

1/4 cup lukewarm water
2 eggs, beaten (optional)
1/4 cup orange juice
2 tablespoons grated orange peel
5 cups flour (about)

Scald milk. Remove from fire and stir in butter or margarine, 1/3 cup sugar, and salt. Cool to lukewarm. Dissolve yeast and 1 teaspoon sugar in lukewarm water. When dissolved and bubbly, stir in the lukewarm milk mixture. Stir in eggs if used, juice, and grated peel. Add enough flour to make a soft dough. Knead on lightly floured breadboard. Put into greased bowl, turning to coat all sides. Cover and let rise until double. Punch down. Knead lightly and roll out to 1/2 inch thick. Make into rolls as desired and place on greased baking sheet. Cover and let rise until double. Bake at 400 degrees for 15 minutes or until golden on top. Top with Orange Glaze. Makes about 2 dozen.

ORANGE GLAZE

2 tablespoons orange juice
1 teaspoon grated orange peel
1 cup sifted powdered sugar

Combine ingredients and glaze hot rolls. These orange rolls can also be made up like cinnamon rolls by rolling dough into rectangles and spreading with a mixture of 1/3 cup soft butter, 1/2 cup sugar, and 2 teaspoons or more of grated orange rind. Roll up and let rise, cut, and continue as directed.

Pudding Mix Sweet Rolls

1 package yeast
1/4 cup lukewarm water
1 box butterscotch pudding mix (not instant)
1 1/2 cups milk

1/2 cup butter or margarine
2 eggs
1 teaspoon salt
4 1/2 to 5 cups flour

Dissolve yeast in lukewarm water. Combine pudding mix, milk, and butter or margarine and cook over low heat, stirring, until thick. Cool to lukewarm. Beat in eggs, salt, and yeast mixture. Add just enough flour to make a soft dough. Knead lightly, place in greased bowl, cover with tea towel, and let rise until double. Divide dough into three parts. Knead slightly, then roll each into a circle, cut into wedges, and put 1 teaspoon of Coconut Filling on each piece. Roll up as for a butterhorn roll, starting at wide end. Place on greased cookie sheet with point of dough underneath. Let rise until double and bake at 375 degrees for 12 to 15 minutes or until golden brown. Glaze while warm if desired. Makes 2 1/2 dozen.

COCONUT FILLING

1/4 cup butter or margarine
2/3 cup brown sugar, packed
2 tablespoons flour

2/3 cup flaked coconut
1/3 cup pecans

Combine ingredients and use as directed.

BUTTERSCOTCH GLAZE

1/4 cup brown sugar, packed
2 tablespoons milk
2 tablespoons butter

1 cup powdered sugar
1/2 teaspoon vanilla flavoring

Combine sugar, milk, and butter. Boil 1 minute. Blend in powdered sugar and flavoring. Glaze hot rolls or frost them when they are cool. This is a delightful butterscotch frosting which can be used on cakes or cookies as well as sweet rolls.

10. Planting

~~~~~~~~~~~~~~~~~~~~~~~~~~~~~~~~~~~~~~
═══════════════════════════════════

Colorful calendars hung in many mid-century farmhouses, compliments of the seed companies, grocery stores, produce houses, and banks in nearby towns. The housewives would hang their copies from nails pounded into the kitchen walls. Above the months and days were pastoral photographs or reproductions of paintings. Brightly patterned wallpaper behind the calendars made for an interesting, though not always artistic, juxtaposition of color and design.

The farmers, in turn, hung their calendars on the walls of the barns, machine sheds, and workshops. The squares on the big pages contained information about such things as weather to come and the best times to plant according to the phases of the moon. The moon-sign dates on the calendar might advise, for example, that vegetables that matured underground should be planted in the dark of the moon and those that bore fruit aboveground should be planted when the moon was nearing fullness. The spaces on the calendars were large enough for the farmers to write down important information such as the days they ordered seeds, planted the fields, had the cows bred, and castrated the pigs.

But no one on the farm really needed a calendar to sense the gradual

*O. F. (Pat) Troxel was one of many farmers
who sold seed corn to supplement their income.
Farragut Forum.*

progression of the year. That could be accurately paced by the activities
of the farm families as they went about their labors.

January found the farmers sitting late in the evening at their kitchen
tables with pads of paper, seed and nursery catalogs, and the measure-
ments of their fields. They figured the cost of the seeds, wrote out the
orders, estimated the number of gallons of fuel to run their machinery,

guessed at the cost for new equipment, then tried to predict the price they would be offered for the harvested crops they would have in nine or ten months if all went well.

In February the farmers were out in the barns and sheds preparing the farrowing spaces and nurseries for the piglets and lambs which were usually born in late winter or early spring. Weather permitting, the farmers repaired machinery, fences, and gates. They loaded hay bales into wagons and pulled them with their tractors to the lots and pastures to feed the cattle. They kept the fires burning in the stock tank water heaters so the animals would have a constant source of drinking water. They scooped manure out of the pig sheds and milking sections of their barns, loaded it into the manure spreaders, and broadcast it onto the fields for fertilizer.

By March a sense of urgency energized the farmers. They tried to guess when the last snow of the winter had arrived and spread clover seed over its white surface to sink into the ground when the snow melted. As soon as the soil was dry enough, the farmers began tilling their fields. First they disked the soil, then harrowed it to smooth out the rough chunks of dirt. They usually planted oats first. The work in the fields often went on from early daylight until dark. In the Midwest this was considered men's work, although several of the women in our neighborhood enjoyed driving the tractors or, for economic reasons, were needed to work in the fields along with the men.

Late April was corn planting time. The farmers used planters that dropped the kernels in rows about 3 1/2 feet apart. Those with land on the flat river bottoms prided themselves on having the straightest, most even rows in the countryside. Robert and the other farmers who worked fields with rolling terrain just planted the seeds in rows as straight as their machinery could put them. Contour planting—following the curving ridges of the field to reduce erosion—was a conservation technique that was yet to come.

When the green spears of corn pushed up from the warm earth a few weeks after the seeds had been planted, the farmers fastened cultivators to their tractors and drove through the fields. The cultivator

Bill Allely fastened his two-row cultivator onto his tractor to dig out the weeds between the corn rows. The shields protected the tiny corn plants from being buried. Ferrell Allely photo.

shovels loosened the soil and plowed out weeds lurking between the rows. Herbicides were not yet in general use, so farmers battled the morning glory vines, thistles, button weeds, and cockleburs by cultivating, hoeing, and pulling. Insecticides were also still in the future, as were most commercial fertilizers. Besides manure from the animals, Robert put anhydrous ammonia on the fields where he felt it would help produce a more abundant crop. Irrigation was not used on southwest Iowa farms, for in normal years, enough rain fell to care for the moisture needs of the growing plants.

Robert purchased his 1948 Ford tractor during the first year on the farm. Wesley and Ray, sons of friends Ed and Eleanor Maynard from Chicago, were fascinated by the farm equipment.

The farmers cultivated their cornfields again in May, in June, and once more in early July. Their goal was to have them "laid by"— cleaned of weeds—no later than the Fourth of July. By then the cornstalks were usually tall and strong enough not to be crowded out by weeds still growing between the rows. Later in the summer, the long leaves of the corn created shade that helped discourage any weeds from sprouting. The corn's height also meant that the tractors and cultivators could no longer navigate the fields without damaging the stalks, so cultivation after mid-July was out of the question.

During hot, humid July days we could almost see the corn pushing higher each day. "Did you hear the corn growing?" Robert would ask on blistering afternoons when he stopped by the house to rinse his perspiring face and to get a glass of iced tea. "It has its own rustling, crackling sound on days like today." Long after he went back into the sun-drenched barnyard, the sweet odors of cornstalks and fresh earth lingered in the kitchen.

Robert's small gray Ford tractor was his primary helper. Depending on the work he needed to do, he would fasten the tractor to his two-bottom plow, planter, harrow, cultivator, mower, wagon, or hayrack. Tractors in the 1940s were not equipped with cabs to protect the farmers from the weather, so Robert and the other farmers had to tolerate spring showers, summer heat, and early winter sleet and cold. They had no radios on their tractors, but the meadowlarks sang to them. The family dogs ran alongside to keep them company. Most farmers developed a sense of kinship with the wild creatures on their land, with the wide blue skies, the brilliant sunshine, the refreshing breezes, and the sweeping view of far horizons. Their pride increased as they rode back and forth across their fields. Whether they owned the land or just tilled it as a renter as Robert did, they felt as if it all belonged to them.

As I worked around the house and yard with my tasks, I liked to hear the sound of the tractor over the hill as Robert made his rounds. The purr of the engine was comforting, and I knew, even though I could not see him, that my husband was not far away.

In the evenings, when their labors were completed, Robert and the other farmers would come back to their barns, take the heavy black wax pencils and mark down on their calendars the work they had completed that day. As the days blended into months and the months into a year, the calendars became diaries of time well spent.

Corn Casserole

1 1-pound can creamed corn
1 1-pound can whole kernel corn
1 cup diced celery
1 cup shredded cheddar cheese

1/4 cup butter or margarine, melted
1 tablespoon dehydrated onion
    (or 1 small onion, chopped)
1 large can onion rings

Combine all ingredients except onion rings. Bake 1 hour at 350 degrees. Top with rings the last half hour of baking time. Makes 6 to 8 servings.

Fried Corn

4 slices bacon
3 cups fresh cut corn (or frozen,
   thawed)

1/4 cup diced sweet green pepper
1/4 cup chopped onion
salt and pepper to taste

Fry out the bacon and remove from skillet. Drain off all but about 3 tablespoons bacon drippings and add remaining ingredients. Cover and cook until corn is just tender—about 6 minutes. Serve hot with crumbled bacon over the top. Makes 6 servings.

Celery Casserole

3 or 4 cups chopped celery
1 8-ounce can sliced water
   chestnuts, drained
1 4-ounce can pimientos, chopped

1 10 3/4-ounce can cream of
   chicken soup
buttered bread crumbs and slivered
   almonds for topping

Boil celery in lightly salted water for 8 minutes. Drain. Combine with remaining ingredients with exception of topping. Top with buttered bread crumbs and slivered almonds. Bake 25 to 30 minutes at 350 degrees, or cover lightly and bake in microwave on high for 5 to 8 minutes. Serves 6.

Creamed Cabbage

1 small head cabbage, shredded
1/4 cup water
2 tablespoons butter or margarine
2 tablespoons flour
1/2 cup milk

1/4 cup half-and-half
1 to 2 tablespoons sugar
1/2 teaspoon salt
1 3-ounce package cream cheese

Combine cabbage and water in covered saucepan. Cook on moderate heat for about 10 minutes or until cabbage is barely tender, stirring occasionally. Add a little more water if needed to keep from scorching. (This can be cooked in the microwave on high for 4 to 6 minutes or until tender.) Drain. Melt butter or margarine in saucepan and stir in flour. When smooth and bubbly, add milk and half-and-half. Continue cooking, stirring, until mixture thickens. Add sugar and salt. Cut cream cheese into chunks and add to cream sauce. Continue cooking over low heat, stirring constantly, until cheese melts. Add sauce to drained cabbage and heat if necessary. This can be made and refrigerated for several hours or overnight and reheated in the microwave just before serving. This cream sauce can be used over other cooked vegetables—asparagus, corn, onions, green beans, broccoli, or carrots. Serves 6 to 8.

Cabbage Slaw for the Freezer

2 cups sugar	1 head cabbage, shredded
1 cup vinegar	2 stalks celery, diced
1/2 cup water	1 sweet red pepper, diced
1/2 teaspoon celery seeds	1 sweet green pepper, diced
1 teaspoon mustard seeds	1 tablespoon pickling salt

Combine sugar, vinegar, water, and celery and mustard seeds. Bring to a boil, stirring to dissolve. Cool. Combine cabbage, celery, and peppers. Sprinkle 1 tablespoon salt over vegetables and let stand 2 hours. Do not drain! Stir in spices and vinegar mixture. Spoon into freezer containers and freeze. When ready to serve, let thaw in refrigerator. Makes 10 to 12 servings.

Carrots with Apricots

3 cups sliced carrots	1/2 cup sour cream or yogurt
1/2 cup diced dried apricots	2 to 3 tablespoons sugar

Slice carrots, add water to cover, and boil until done. Wash dried apricots and dice. Cover with boiling water and set aside to soak for 5 minutes. Drain carrots and apricots and combine. Just before serving, toss with sour cream or yogurt and mix with sugar to taste. Serve cold or heat just slightly (do not boil) and serve hot. This can also be made with canned carrots, heated and drained. Fresh or frozen carrots are easy to cook in the microwave with just a little moisture for 4 minutes on high or until tender. Serves 5.

Cucumbers in Yogurt Dressing

8 ounces plain yogurt
1 clove garlic, minced
2 tablespoons lemon juice
2 tablespoons olive oil

1 teaspoon sugar
dash of salt
cucumbers

Combine everything with exception of cucumbers. Peel and chop cucumbers into a bowl until you have as many as you wish. Toss lightly with dressing and refrigerate until time to serve. Garnish with mint leaves. Serves 6 to 8.

Elegant Peas

4 cups frozen peas
4 lettuce leaves
10 green onions, sliced
2 teaspoons sugar
1/4 teaspoon thyme

1 small bay leaf
1 teaspoon parsley flakes
2 tablespoons butter or margarine
1/2 cup cold water
salt to taste

Combine ingredients in a heavy saucepan. Cover top of pan with heat-proof pie plate and fill this plate half full of cold water. Cook over moderate heat until peas are tender, about 10 minutes. The cold water in the pie plate causes the steam inside to condense and drop back onto the cooking peas, eliminating the need for a larger amount of liquid. If the water in the pie pan evaporates, add more. This recipe can also be prepared in the microwave. Combine ingredients, cover with plastic wrap, and microwave on high for 5 to 6 minutes. Makes 8 servings.

Vegetable Pizza

2 8-ounce packages crescent rolls	1 teaspoon minced onion
2 8-ounce packages cream cheese, softened	1 1/2 cups fresh chopped broccoli
2/3 cup mayonnaise	1 1/2 cups grated carrots
1 teaspoon dill weed	1 1/2 cups fresh diced cauliflower
1/4 teaspoon garlic powder	1 cup thinly sliced radishes

Roll out crescent dough to fit a 15-by-10-inch jelly roll pan and place it gently in the pan. Bake 15 minutes at 375 degrees or until light brown. Combine cream cheese, mayonnaise, dill weed, garlic powder, and onion. Spread over baked layer. Sprinkle chopped vegetables over the top, cover lightly with waxed paper, and refrigerate at least 2 hours before serving. This pizza can be cut into small pieces and served as an appetizer. Serves 12 to 24, depending on size of pieces.

Wilted Greens

6 slices bacon	3 tablespoons vinegar
2 tablespoons minced onion or shallots	2 tablespoons water
1 tablespoon sugar or honey	salt and pepper to taste

Fry out bacon in skillet then remove to small bowl. Drain off all but 4 tablespoons of bacon drippings and sauté onion or shallots in hot fat until golden. Add remaining ingredients to skillet. When hot, pour over about 4 cups washed and dried greens—lettuce leaves, spinach, arugula, etc. Toss lightly. Crumble bacon over top. Makes 4 servings.

Stuffed Zucchini

4 medium zucchini	1/2 cup bread crumbs
2 tablespoons oil	1/4 cup grated cheese
1 small onion, minced	2 tablespoons parsley
2 eggs, lightly beaten	salt and pepper to taste

Cut zucchini in half lengthwise. Scoop out pulp, leaving the shell. Simmer in boiling salted water for 2 minutes to soften. Drain and set aside to cool. Chop zucchini pulp and onion into a skillet with the oil. Sauté until transparent. Remove from heat and combine with remaining ingredients. Fill shells. Place on greased baking dish and bake at 375 degrees for about 15 minutes or until heated through. This is also a good stuffing for tomatoes. Makes 4 to 6 servings.

11. Haying

~~~~~~~~~~~~~~~~~~~~~

By June the fields of alfalfa and red clover had spread a fresh green cloak over the land, sending up a pungent fragrance that delighted people and bees alike. On the farms of southwest Iowa, it was time to put up hay.

Farmers could not afford to waste a minute when the haying began. The legumes had to be mowed, then raked, dried, and stored in the barns before an unexpected shower could make the crop wet and moldy. Moist hay piled in the haymow of a barn could heat up to the point of spontaneously bursting into flames, so drying it before storage was essential. Farm folks were always apprehensive about the possibility of rain when several acres of their alfalfa or clover were cut and drying on the ground. "The hay is down," they would say. "Time to worry about the weather."

Clover produced only one crop a year, but alfalfa kept growing all summer. Three times a year—four if it was an especially good growing year—the farmers would drive their tractors and mowers out to their fields to cut the tall green stalks. They left them to dry for twenty-four hours, then combed the fields with tractor-pulled rakes which left the hay in neat windrows. After the sun had dried the hay a bit more, they baled it and hauled it to the barns.

Martin Schnoor would bring his hay baler over from his farm and bale our hay. This field was one of my favorite places on the farm. It had a view of rolling hills in the distance and a nearby spring-fed brook.

Some farmers had their own balers. Others hired a neighbor with machinery to custom bale their alfalfa and clover. In our case it was Jake Schnoor's son, Martin, who came to our assistance. His baler was an ingenious machine that scooped up the loose windrows of hay, compressed them into sixty-pound rectangular bales, tied each one with twine or wire, then pushed it out onto the ground.

After Martin baled the hay, he headed for home. While I drove the tractor pulling the hayrack, Robert lifted the bales by hand and stacked them in neat rows on the flat wooden wagon. High boards at the back of the hayrack gave stability to the first rows of bales, and Robert fit the rest in front of them. While we worked, our children rode on the wagon or played among the trees on the grass-covered bank of the brook out of the way of the machinery.

When the rack was full, the youngsters and I climbed up to sprawl on top of the bales while Robert turned the tractor and wagon toward the barn. We smelled the rich fragrant hay beneath us, watched the broad blue sky filled with fleecy clouds above us, felt the warm sun shining down on us, and held hands all the way to the barn.

I drove the tractor as Robert loaded bales on the hay wagon. Visitors to the farm liked to help. On the hay wagon are niece Luanne and nephew Larry Barnard of Omaha, and to the right, our son, Bob.

Once the children were safely inside the fenced yard, Robert and I unloaded the bales into the hayloft. Robert drove the large prongs of a hayfork into the bales, then I inched the tractor forward, pulling a rope that lifted the fork and its load up and through a door high on the barn. When Robert pulled the trip rope that opened the hayfork, the bales tumbled into the loft. I eased the tractor backward while Robert lowered the hayfork back down to the wagon and clamped it onto the next load of hay.

The hottest part of the work for us was going up into the loft to make order out of the randomly dropped bales. As we pushed and stacked the bales in neat rows, the temperature under the eaves of the barn was often above one hundred degrees. Perspiration ran over our bodies, and the prickly bits of hay drifted down our shirts, into our socks, and around our waists. It was a relief to get the job done and

Robert used the hayfork to lift the hay into the barn loft. Looking out the window to the right are Larry and Luanne Barnard, Dulcie Jean, and Bob. The lower level of the barn was a safe area for the children.

hurry to the house to drop our sticky clothes on the back porch and head for a wash under the windmill in the tubs filled with sun-warmed water.

In addition to driving the tractor, I made sure my family and any neighbors who came to help with the haying had good meals. I had to plan ahead so the food could be prepared as quickly as possible. I fixed snacks to carry along in a cooler, and the best part of many of those days were the picnic dinners we shared in the field. Our evening meal was always a sturdy supper based on dishes that I prepared and stored in the refrigerator a day or two before haying began. As soon as the family was washed and into clean clothes, Robert headed back to the barn to do the milking while I got the food onto the table. Later in the evening, as we sat together to eat, we were grateful that one more cutting of hay was safely stored in the barn.

Putting up hay was long, tiring work, but we had a tremendous sense of accomplishment each time the task was finished. We might be slaves to the seasons, the weather, and the needs of the livestock, but if anyone had asked us, we would have insisted that we enjoyed a greater independence and felt less restricted on the farm than we ever had in any other occupation.

Hay Hand Rolls

1 package yeast	1 cup melted shortening or salad oil
1 cup lukewarm water	1 cup sugar or honey
1 teaspoon sugar	3 eggs, beaten (optional)
3 cups lukewarm water	2 to 3 teaspoons salt
4 cups flour	10 cups flour (about)

In a large bowl combine yeast, 1 cup lukewarm water, and 1 teaspoon sugar. Let stand about 5 minutes until yeast is dissolved and mixture is bubbly. Add 3 cups more lukewarm water and 4 cups flour. Beat until batter is full of bubbles. Cover and let this "sponge" set for several hours or overnight. Stir down several times. Add shortening or oil, sugar or honey, eggs (if you use them), salt, and enough flour to make a soft dough. Turn out on floured breadboard and knead for about 5 minutes or until smooth and elastic (dough has a springy feel). Do not add any more flour than necessary for light rolls. Put into greased bowl, cover, and let rise in a draft-free place until double. A cool oven with a pan of hot water in the bottom is an excellent place for yeast doughs to rise. Punch dough down and cut into two or three portions. Knead each portion and make out into rolls. Place in greased baking pans, cover with clean tea towels, and let rise until double. Bake at 375 degrees for 20 to 30 minutes or until golden brown on top. This is an excellent refrigerator dough. The small amount of yeast keeps it from becoming "sour" during storage. Cover dough with a plate or lid and it will keep in the refrigerator up to a week. Remove amount of dough desired from refrigerator and let warm to room temperature for at least 1 hour, then proceed as directed. This recipe came from a farm wife who made it often for the men who came to help put up hay. Makes 3 to 4 dozen rolls, depending on size.

Triple Fudge Brownies

1 box chocolate pudding mix (not instant)
1 regular-sized box chocolate cake mix

1 teaspoon vanilla flavoring
chocolate chips and chopped nuts (optional)

Cook the pudding mix according to directions. Cool slightly. While still warm, mix with dry cake mix. Beat in flavoring. Mix well—be certain all the dry ingredients are dissolved into the pudding mix. Grease and flour a 9-by-13-inch baking pan, spoon in batter. Top with chocolate chips and nuts if desired. Bake according to directions on cake mix box. The top is shiny when it is done, so best test with a toothpick inserted in the middle. This makes a heavy, cakelike brownie and is a fine brownie to take out to the field for snacks. Makes about 15 squares.

Exquisite Chocolate Cake

3/4 cup butter
2 1/4 cups sugar
1 1/2 teaspoons vanilla flavoring
3 eggs
3 squares unsweetened chocolate, melted

3 cups sifted cake flour
1 1/2 teaspoons baking soda
3/4 teaspoon salt
1 1/2 cups ice water

Blend butter, sugar, and flavoring together in mixing bowl until smooth and creamy. Add eggs and continue beating until mixture is light and fluffy. Melt chocolate, cool slightly, and stir in. Sift dry ingredients together and add to batter alternately with ice water. Grease three 8- or 9-inch layer cake pans and line with waxed or baking paper. Pour in the batter and bake in a 350-degree oven for 30 to 35 minutes. This cake freezes well. Makes about 20 servings.

DATE-NUT FILLING

1 cup milk

1/2 cup chopped dates

1/4 cup sugar

1 tablespoon flour

1 egg, beaten

1 1/2 cups chopped nuts

1 teaspoon vanilla flavoring

Combine milk and dates in top of double boiler. Set over hot water and heat. Mix sugar, flour, and egg together and gradually blend into date mixture. Cook, stirring often, until mixture thickens. Remove from fire and stir in nuts and flavoring. Cool and spread between layers of chocolate cake. Frost with Fudge Frosting.

FUDGE FROSTING

1 cup sugar

1 egg

1 square unsweetened chocolate,
  grated (or 2 level tablespoons
  cocoa)

1/2 tablespoon butter

3 tablespoons cream

1 teaspoon vanilla flavoring

Combine ingredients in heavy saucepan, bring to a boil, and boil for 3 minutes. Let cool for a short time and then beat to spreading consistency. Frost top and sides of cake.

Red-hot Apple Roll

1 1/2 cups sugar

1 1/2 cups water

1/2 cup red-hot candies

3 cups peeled chopped apples

2 cups flour

2 teaspoons baking powder

1/2 teaspoon salt

1/4 cup sugar

1/3 cup shortening

1 egg

milk to make 2/3 cup liquid

1 to 2 tablespoons butter or
    margarine, softened

Combine sugar, water, and candies, Bring to a boil and simmer for 5 minutes to dissolve candies. Reserve 1/2 cup of the syrup for the topping and pour the rest into a 9-by-12-inch baking pan. Peel and chop the apples into salted water to keep from darkening; set aside while you make the biscuit dough. Combine dry ingredients. Cut in shortening. Break the egg into a measuring cup and add enough milk to make 2/3 cup liquid. Beat with a fork to combine. Add to flour mixture and stir just enough to moisten ingredients and dough clings together in a ball. Knead lightly on a pastry cloth or floured breadboard for 10 to 12 strokes and then roll out to a rectangle. Spread with 1 or 2 tablespoons of soft butter or margarine and cover with chopped, drained apples. Roll up like a jelly roll and slice. Lay slices on red cinnamon syrup in pan. Bake at 400 degrees for 30 minutes. Spoon reserved syrup, 1 tablespoon for each roll, over the top. Return to oven and bake 10 minutes longer or until brown. Elegant served with whipped cream or whipped topping. This can also be made with a mincemeat filling for an entirely different taste delight. Serves 12.

Fried Apples

4 large apples

3 tablespoons butter

1/3 cup water

1/3 cup sugar

dash of salt

Slice apples into skillet with melted butter. Add remaining ingredients, cover, and cook gently, stirring occasionally, for about 4 minutes or until apples are tender. Uncover and continue cooking, stirring a bit, until syrup thickens. Serve as a meat accompaniment or as a dessert.

Cinnamon or Mint Apple Rings

1/2 cup sugar

1 cup water

1/4 cup white corn syrup

1/4 cup red-hot candies

1/8 teaspoon red food coloring

5 or 6 firm cooking apples, cored
   and sliced

Combine sugar, water, corn syrup, and candies. Cook about 4 minutes to dissolve candies. Add food coloring as desired. Place apples in syrup and continue simmering for about 10 minutes or until tender and transparent. Turn slices several times. Cool in syrup. You can make green mint apple rings by eliminating red-hot candies and using a little green food coloring and 1 teaspoon mint flavoring. Makes about 25 rings.

Baked Apples

Cut off a 24-inch strip of aluminum foil for each apple. Fold the foil in half and place a cored apple in the center. Fill the hole with 1 tablespoon red-hot candies, 1 tablespoon raisins, and 1 teaspoon butter or margarine. Wrap foil around each apple and twist the ends to seal. Bake at 425 degrees for about 30 minutes or until tender. Fold down foil and serve in the little foil container. This can also be done in the microwave. Use plastic wrap in place of foil and place each apple in a small saucer or Pyrex bowl. Microwave on high for 5 minutes, rotating saucer once. Test for doneness. Make as many as you want.

12. Harvesting

In the pioneer days of harvesting in the Midwest, farmers cut their wheat and oats and stacked the long stalks in tepee-shaped shocks. The grain dried for two or three weeks, then crews brought in big coal-fired threshing machines to separate the grain from the straw. By the 1940s and 1950s in our area, shocks of grain and huge threshing machines were things of the past. Country folks harvested their wheat and oats with combines that cut, threshed, and cleaned the grain during one pass across the field. The combines spewed the grain into wagons and tossed the straw onto the ground where farmers could bale it later for use as bedding for livestock. Almost everyone had their wheat and oats combined and stored in the grain bins by the end of August.

September was fruit harvest time, and farmers with large orchards, like Ed Nelson, put every member of their families to work bringing in the crop. They stored several bushels of fruit in their cellars for winter use, then sorted the rest into baskets for sale. The less perfect apples were made into cider.

Corn picking usually began in October when the stalks and ears were dry. The corn pickers were great, noisy machines that could be identified by color. John Deere equipment was traditionally bright

An Allis-Chalmers corn picker in 1950. Shenandoah Evening Sentinel *photo.*

green, Oliver olive green, Case yellow, Wood Brothers gray, International Harvester red, Massey Harris crimson red, Allis-Chalmers orange, and New Idea had a silvery metallic finish. Corn pickers were expensive, so farmers who purchased them for their own use often traded labor or contracted to harvest corn for their neighbors who did not own pickers. Robert went to Jake and Martin Schnoor's farms to help with their harvest, then Martin brought his corn picker to our farm and helped Robert with his.

Some corn pickers were designed to be pulled behind a tractor, while some styles could be mounted on a tractor. As this mechanical marvel moved through the rows of corn, its mechanism pulled the ears into snapping rollers that removed the ears from the stalks, rolling off the dry shucks in the process. After the field was picked, the cattle and hogs were herded in to glean any kernels or tasty leaves left on the ground.

Our corncrib was rectangular, built of boards nailed several inches apart so the air could circulate around the stored ears to dry the kernels. The crib had galvanized metal sheets for a roof, which Robert could remove when he was ready to unload his wagons of corn.

Bob Troxel pulled a wagon filled with corn close to his crib and positioned the front wheels on a platform hoist. As his son, Jeff, watched, Bob unhooked the wagon from the tractor, turned on the engine connecting it to the hoist, and raised up the wagon. He would then open the tailgate and the ears of corn would tumble out and onto the belt of the elevator. It, in turn, lifted the corn up to the spout that aimed the grain into the crib. Bob Troxel photo.

Robert pulled each filled wagon from the field to the barnyard and used an auger and elevator to lift the ears into the crib. The work was easy until the crib was almost full, then he had to push the spout of the elevator back and forth to get the corn into every corner. As the pile grew higher, Robert sometimes climbed into the crib to kick the ears around to level them out and fill the space evenly. During the winter, he fed the corn to the livestock or had it shelled off the cob and sold to the grain storage elevator in Farragut. He kept a supply of the dry cobs in a shed to burn as fuel in the stock tank heaters in the winter.

Almost every part of corn picking was dangerous. If farmers tried to pull tangled stalks out of the machinery while it was running (it was easier to remove them while the rollers were turning than when they

Left to right: Terry, Ronny, and Monica Allely. Ferrell Allely photo.

were still), their fingers, hands, or arms could be caught and mangled. The tumbling rods that ran from the tractor engine to the auger to move the elevators could snag a sleeve or pant leg and quickly wrench off an arm or leg. More than a few farm workers were killed in harvesting accidents.

While her husband toiled in the fields, the farm wife was anything but idle. She prepared large noon dinners and kept the workers supplied with sandwiches, jugs or fruit jars of water, and thermos bottles filled with hot coffee and tea.

The harvest meals I cooked during my years on the farm were not as enormous as those prepared by women in earlier days for the threshing and corn-picking crews, but hungry workers are hungry workers regardless of their number, so I peeled and chopped, stewed and fried, mixed and baked. Since only one or two neighbors were involved in our harvesting operations, I did all the cooking and serving by myself, but I heard many stories about times when larger numbers of men were helping one another and their wives came along to pitch in with the cooking, serving, and cleanup.

I was introduced to such a cooperative experience on a blustery day in November of 1951 when ten corn pickers descended upon the Allely farm just a few miles north of our country lane. They were followed by tractors pulling wagons and by cars full of farm families. A neighborhood gathering was often a time of celebration and joy, but this occasion was filled with sadness and an intensity of purpose. Six weeks earlier, Bill Allely had died after undergoing emergency heart surgery. He was only thirty-six years old and left his wife, Ferrell, and their three young children, Ronny, Monica, and Terry.

The crops that Bill had planted had ripened, and the neighbors were joining together to bring in the harvest. Their willingness to help was a display of respect for Bill as surely as had been their attendance at his funeral. The farmers fanned out across the fields with their machinery, hauling in the corn and elevating it into the bins. At noon they drove into the barnyard and parked their tractors and wagons in rows along the fence. Then they came to the back door where the women had put out pails of water, wash pans, soap, and towels so the dusty workers could clean up for the midday meal.

The Allely house was rich with the aroma of fried chicken and baked ham. A line of freshly baked pies cooled on the back porch table. Ferrell inserted extra leaves in her dining room table and spread it with her best white tablecloth. We loaded it with platters of meat and bowls of mashed potatoes, gravy, and vegetables. After we put out baskets of hot homemade rolls and filled the coffee cups, dinner was ready.

There wasn't room at the table for all the men to sit at once, so they came in shifts. How they ate! We kept refilling the bowls and platters, poured more coffee and water, and served big slices of pie. After all the men had eaten and returned to their work, we women sat at the long table and ate our own meal.

It was at that moment that I realized that my family and I had truly become part of the farm community. I was glad to be living in a place where there was such cooperation, both in good times and in bad. As we came together to help with another family's harvest, we were doing more than just picking corn and baking pies. We were bringing encouragement to a family in trouble and strengthening our own friendships.

Traditional Pie Crust

2 cups flour
1/2 teaspoon baking powder
  (optional)

1/2 teaspoon salt
1 cup lard or vegetable shortening
1/2 cup cold water

Combine dry ingredients and cut in cold lard or shortening with two knives or a pastry blender until mixture resembles coarse crumbs. Gradually add cold water until mixture can be shaped into a ball. Roll out as needed. Makes enough for 4 single-crust or 2 double-crust pies.

Freezer Pie Crust

3 cups flour
1 1/4 cups vegetable shortening
1/4 teaspoon salt

1 egg or 2 egg whites, lightly beaten
1 teaspoon vinegar
5 or 6 tablespoons cold water

Cut flour, shortening, and salt together with two knives or a pastry blender. Combine egg, vinegar, and water and mix into flour mixture with a fork. Press dough together in waxed paper or plastic to form a ball. Chill about 15 minutes. Take a portion at a time and roll out about 1/8 inch thick. This dough can be made ahead, rolled out, wrapped in plastic, and frozen until time to use. Most unbaked fruit pies freeze well if wrapped carefully. Unwrap and put into oven frozen. Add a little more baking time for the frozen pies. Makes enough for 5 single-crust or 2 double-crust pies.

Apple Pie

1 double-crust pie shell
3/4 cup sugar
4 tablespoons flour or cornstarch
dash of salt
1/2 teaspoon cinnamon

4 to 5 cups peeled, thinly sliced
    cooking apples
3 tablespoons milk or half-and-half
2 tablespoons butter (optional)

Prepare 1 double-crust pie shell. Combine dry ingredients. Mix in the peeled and sliced apples. Arrange bottom crust in 9-inch pie pan. Sprinkle about 1 tablespoon of flour over the crust or brush with lightly beaten egg white to keep it from getting soggy. Spoon apple mixture into unbaked pie shell. Sprinkle milk or half-and-half over the top of the apples and dot with butter if desired. Arrange top crust. Be sure and make slits in the top crust to let out the steam. Bake at 425 degrees for about 10 minutes, then lower heat to 350 degrees and continue baking for about 30 minutes until nicely brown and apples are tender. If edges brown too fast, make a collar with aluminum foil and cover edges, continue baking as directed. Delicious served with ice cream or slices of yellow cheese. A half cup cheddar cheese can be grated into the apple mixture before baking for an interesting variation.

Harvester's Cobbler

1 recipe pie crust
3 cups sugar
3/4 cup flour

pinch of salt
2 quarts fresh pitted cherries
2 tablespoons butter or margarine

Prepare pie crust. Combine sugar, flour, and salt. Pour over the cherries and mix well. Put into two 9-by-13-inch baking pans. Dot with butter. Roll out pie crust in rectangles large enough to cover top of pans. Pull crust over the top of the cherries to very edge. Sprinkle the crust with a little cream or milk and sprinkle a little sugar over top for sparkle. Bake at 400 degrees for 30 minutes or until top is nicely browned and cherries have cooked and thickened. (They thicken more as they cool.) This was a fast way to prepare a big dessert for harvesters. Served with ice cream, it was a real treat. Other fruits may be used but you may want to use less sugar than for the sour fresh cherries. Makes lots!

Rhubarb and Strawberry Pie

1 double-crust pie shell
4 cups diced rhubarb
2 cups sugar

dash of salt
4 tablespoons minute tapioca
1 cup sliced strawberries

Prepare 1 double-crust pie shell. Wash and dice rhubarb. Measure 4 cups into a large bowl and stir in sugar, salt, and tapioca. Wash and stem strawberries and slice into rhubarb mixture. Line a 9-inch pie pan with crust and sprinkle with about 1 tablespoon flour or brush with lightly beaten egg white to help keep it from soaking up the filling. Spoon fruit mixture into unbaked pie shell, put on top crust, and bake at 400 degrees for about 30 to 40 minutes or until top is brown and mixture is bubbling out of steam vents in crust.

Pineapple Pie

1 double-crust pie shell
3 cups crushed pineapple
2/3 cup pineapple juice and water

3/4 cup sugar
4 tablespoons minute tapioca

Prepare 1 double-crust pie shell. Drain pineapple and measure syrup into cup. Add water if needed to make 2/3 cup. Combine all ingredients and set aside for 15 minutes. Arrange bottom crust in 9-inch pie pan. Spoon pineapple filling into unbaked pie shell and dot with butter if desired. Arrange top crust and bake at 400 degrees for about 40 minutes or until golden brown.

Easy Chocolate Pie

1 baked single-crust pie shell
2 cups milk
3/4 cup sugar
3 tablespoons cocoa
1/2 teaspoon salt

3 egg yolks
2 tablespoons butter
1 teaspoon vanilla flavoring
meringue

Prepare 1 single-crust pie shell. Mix together milk, sugar, cocoa, and salt. Cook in top of double boiler over boiling water or in a heavy pan over moderate heat. Cook, stirring constantly, until mixture starts to thicken. Beat the egg yolks and blend a little of the hot mixture into the yolks to warm (so they don't cook when they hit the chocolate mixture), then gradually stir the egg yolks into hot filling. Add butter and flavoring, and keep simmering, stirring, for 2 minutes or until mixture is thick. Remove from heat, cool slightly, and pour into baked 9-inch pie shell. Top with meringue, sealing to edges. Bake in 350-degree oven until golden brown, about 15 minutes. Serves 6 to 8.

Meringue

3 egg whites
1/4 teaspoon cream of tartar
7 tablespoons sugar

Beat egg whites and cream of tartar together until frothy. Continue beating, gradually adding the sugar, until sugar is dissolved and egg whites form firm peaks. (Taste a little of the meringue. It should not be gritty if the sugar is well dissolved.) Spread over top of pie, sealing to edges.

Lemon Meringue Pie

1 baked single-crust pie shell
1 cup sugar
3 tablespoons cornstarch
3 tablespoons flour
dash of salt
1 1/2 cups hot water

3 egg yolks, lightly beaten
2 tablespoons butter
1/3 cup lemon juice
1/2 teaspoon grated lemon peel
meringue

Prepare 1 single-crust pie shell. Combine sugar, cornstarch, flour, and salt. Add hot water and mix well. Boil over moderate heat, stirring constantly, until it begins to thicken. Stir small amount of hot mixture into egg yolks, return to hot mixture in pan. Boil 2 minutes. Remove from heat. Add butter, lemon juice, and lemon peel. Cool slightly. Prepare meringue. Pour filling into baked 9-inch pie shell, top with meringue, and bake at 400 degrees until golden brown on top.

Crumble-top Peach Pie

1 single-crust pie shell
1 cup sugar
1/3 cup butter

1/4 cup flour
6 to 8 peaches, peeled and sliced
4 tablespoons cream

Prepare 1 single-crust pie shell. Cream together sugar, butter, and flour until crumbly. Place half this creamed mixture on bottom of the unbaked 9-inch pie shell. Slice peaches over top. (Frozen or canned drained fruit can also be used.) Top the peaches with remaining crumbly mixture. Sprinkle cream over the top. Bake at 350 degrees until golden brown. Serve plain or with ice cream or whipped cream.

Strawberry Pie

1 baked single-crust pie shell
1 1/2 quarts strawberries
3/4 cup sugar

3 tablespoons cornstarch
1/2 cup water
1 tablespoon butter or margarine

Prepare 1 single-crust pie shell. Wash and drain berries. Remove stems. Crush enough to make 1 cup. Combine sugar and cornstarch. Add crushed berries and water. Cook over medium heat, stirring constantly, until mixture boils and becomes thick and clear. Remove from heat, stir in butter, and cool. Place remaining whole berries in baked 9-inch pie shell. Pour cooled sauce over berries. Chill at least 2 hours. Top with whipped cream or whipped topping that has been sweetened slightly and flavored with vanilla. Garnish with pretty, whole strawberries. This pie may also be made using peaches.

Grape Pie

1 double-crust pie shell
2 pounds Concord grapes

3/4 cup sugar
1 1/2 tablespoons flour

Prepare 1 double-crust pie shell. Pull grapes from stems and wash well. Slip skins into a bowl. Put pulp in a saucepan. Cook until soft and seeds begin to separate. Run cooked pulp through a sieve or a food mill to remove seeds. Let the pulp go into the bowl with the skins. Discard seeds. Measure out 2 cups of the skin-pulp mixture and add sugar and flour. Spoon into bottom of unbaked 9-inch pie shell and top with second crust or cover with lattice top. Bake at 400 degrees for 10 minutes. Reduce heat to 350 degrees and bake for another 25 to 30 minutes. If edges brown too rapidly, make a collar of aluminum foil to protect the crust. The grape filling can be prepared and frozen in individual pie-sized portions.

13. Country Social Clubs

Farm women worked so many long hours at home that they ordinarily did not have time to drive back and forth to visit their neighbors for morning coffee, afternoon tea, or casual encounters. Their social contacts focused on Saturday evening trips to town, working on church projects, Sundays spent with relatives, and attending an occasional auction sale. Among the most enjoyable opportunities to visit, however, were the meetings of the country social clubs, which the members took turns holding in their homes.

Each monthly gathering gave farm wives a chance to sit quietly for a few hours, when sitting was a luxury for most. It provided a sense of companionship at a time when many rural women worked alone or had only small children as their daytime companions. The preschool children came with their mothers and played with one another, so the meetings were always lively and often downright noisy. The women shared information about subjects that were important to them. They discussed the books they were reading, their favorite recipes, laundry and house-cleaning hints, how their gardens were growing, the current price of farm produce, the cost of seeds and fertilizers, and the best way to care for their children.

The Friendly Fairview Club occasionally met at the Fairview schoolhouse. Marjorie Hayes-Donaldson photo.

Some of the clubs were named for the geographical areas that had once comprised country school districts. My sister, Ruth Bricker, Fair and Marilyn Troxel, Marge Schnoor, and other women north of Cottonwood Farm belonged to the Centennial Club, named for the Centennial School District. Along with my closest neighbors, I belonged to the Friendly Fairview Club in the old Fairview School District.

The clubs began in various ways and at different times. The Lone Willow Birthday Club in the old Lone Willow School District had started with the delightful idea of going to a member's home on her birthday and taking refreshments, cards, and gifts. It outgrew its original purpose, discontinued the birthday celebrations, and became a fellowship group similar to the other societies.

The B.B. Club was organized in 1900 by twelve young women who played baseball and basketball together. As the members grew in age and numbers, their interests shifted to homemaking and fellowship. The Mothers' Study Club was started in 1917 by five mothers with

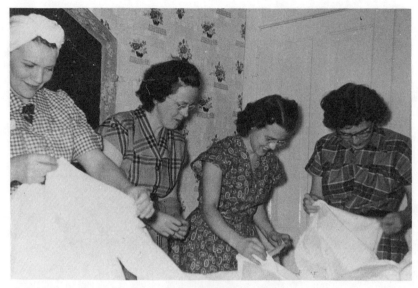

The country women undertook sewing projects for worthwhile causes. These women are making choir robes.

young children. Its purpose, as written in their yearbook, was "to awaken a deeper sense of the responsibility as mothers and to bring about conditions under which children may develop mentally, morally, and physically to their fullest extent." As more ladies joined, and as the children grew older, the members launched into studies on many subjects—health, religion, music, art, travel, and character building. The O.N.O. Club—"Our Night Out"—offered women an opportunity to get away from family responsibilities one evening a month for general study and recreational gatherings.

As soon as a new family moved into their territory, members of the local organization knocked on the farmhouse kitchen door to invite any adult women in the household to be a part of their group. No one, as far as I know, was ever left out of this welcoming tradition.

The activities of the clubs were diverse. Members held showers for new brides and, later, for their babies. They took food to families suffering from illness, accident, or death. They collected clothing for a family after a fire destroyed their house and belongings and prepared Christmas gift boxes for orphanages. These women did many similar

The Centennial Club women dressed up like hoboes for a fun meeting. Marilyn Troxel photo.

projects in their churches, but the social clubs offered a different mix of backgrounds, religious affiliations, and ages to give distinctiveness to the women's efforts.

The club members had fun, too, enjoying potluck dinners, picnics, luncheons, and gift exchanges. Several groups included Mystery Pals in their entertainment. Each member drew the name of another and sent that person small surprise gifts on holidays and birthdays and for special events. The identities of Mystery Pals were revealed at the final session of the year.

Meetings were not without their struggles. The hostess for the month cleaned her house, prepared refreshments, prayed that her children would stay well, and hoped that in the middle of the meeting her husband would not need to ask her to drive into town to get parts for a broken piece of farm machinery. I was especially pleased when it didn't rain on the days I entertained the Friendly Fairview Club. If it did, the ladies could drive along the gravel road only as far as our mailbox, then Robert would use his tractor to pull their cars up our long, muddy lane.

Whether it was my own Friendly Fairview Club, the Centennial

Club, the Better Homes Club, the Friendly Fu, the Sunshine Club, the Happy Homemakers, the Boosters, the Best Ever, or any of the other southwest Iowa organizations, every hostess tried to serve her best salad or dessert for refreshments. The finest compliment she could receive was when the other members asked her to share the recipe with them. Out came pencils and papers from purses as the hostess, her face beaming, handed around the recipe to be copied. I was grateful for those sharing sessions, for they provided me with excellent recipes to use in my columns. Many a husband was grateful as well, for the various foods that graced his meals were often the result of those country social club gatherings.

Two-Layer Club Salad

FIRST LAYER

1 3-ounce package lemon gelatin
1 cup boiling water

1 1/2 cups cottage cheese,
   undrained

Dissolve gelatin in boiling water. Cool slightly and whip until light and fluffy; add cottage cheese. Pour into mold or glass pan. Chill until firm.

SECOND LAYER

1 3-ounce package lime gelatin
1 cup boiling water
1 cup pineapple juice
1 cup canned pineapple chunks

1/3 cup stuffed olives, sliced
1/3 cup chopped pecans or English
   walnuts

Dissolve gelatin in boiling water. Stir in pineapple juice. Cool and add remaining ingredients. Spoon over bottom layer. Chill until time to serve. Cut into squares or unmold on lettuce leaves. Makes up to 15 servings.

Orange Sherbet Salad

1 3-ounce package orange gelatin
mandarin orange juice, heated
2 cups orange sherbet

1 11-ounce can mandarin oranges,
*   drained*
bananas (optional)

Dissolve gelatin in hot juice. Stir in sherbet and oranges. Add bananas if desired. Pour into an 8-by-8-inch dish or a pretty bowl. Chill. Garnish with mandarin orange slices. Serve either as a salad or as a dessert. Makes up to 8 servings.

Red Raspberry Salad

FIRST LAYER

1 6-ounce package red raspberry
*   gelatin (or 2 3-ounce packages)*
2 cups boiling water
1/2 cup cold water

2 tablespoons lemon juice
1 1/2 cups applesauce
2 10-ounce packages frozen red
*   raspberries*

Dissolve gelatin in boiling water. Stir in remaining ingredients, including juice from raspberries. When well mixed, pour into a 9-by-13-inch pan. Chill.

TOPPING

1 cup sour cream or plain yogurt
15 large marshmallows, diced

Combine ingredients and let stand at room temperature until marshmallows are soft. Spread over firm bottom layer and refrigerate until time to serve. Miniature marshmallows can be used in place of large ones. Makes 15 servings.

Blueberry Salad

1 6-ounce package grape gelatin (or
   2 3-ounce packages)
3 cups boiling water

1 21-ounce can blueberry pie mix
   (or 2 cups fresh blueberries)
small can crushed pineapple,
   undrained

Dissolve gelatin in boiling water. Cool until syrupy. Add blueberry pie filling or washed and drained fresh blueberries and pineapple. Pour into 9-by-13-inch pan. Chill until firm. Add topping. Serves 15.

TOPPING

1 8-ounce package cream cheese,
   softened
1 8-ounce carton sour cream

1/4 cup sugar
1 teaspoon vanilla
1/2 cup nuts (optional)

Soften cream cheese to room temperature, then combine with remaining ingredients. Mix well and spread over salad. Chill. Cut into squares and serve on lettuce leaves.

Black Cherry Salad

1 3-ounce package cherry gelatin
1 cup boiling water
1 cup cherry juice and water

1 cup black cherries, pitted
1/4 cup chopped nuts
1/2 cup diced celery

Dissolve gelatin in boiling water. Drain cherry juice into measuring cup and add enough water to make 1 cup, then stir into dissolved gelatin. Fold in remaining ingredients and spoon into individual salad molds or pretty glass bowl. Chill until firm. Unmold or serve in bowl with 1/4 cup mayonnaise combined with 1/2 cup whipped topping on the side.

Broccoli Salad

3 stalks broccoli, washed and
   chopped
1 small red onion, diced
6 slices bacon, fried crisp and
   crumbled

1/2 cup raisins
1/2 cup chopped nuts
1/2 cup mayonnaise
1 teaspoon sugar
1 teaspoon vinegar

Put first five ingredients in a bowl. Combine remaining ingredients and toss into first mixture. Refrigerate for several hours or overnight. Keeps well for several days. Serve with crispy crackers or finger sandwiches. This is a wonderful recipe to make ahead for club meetings or for other gatherings. Makes 10 servings.

Tuna Crunch Salad

1 6 1/8-ounce can tuna fish,
   drained
1/3 cup chopped sweet pickles
3 tablespoons minced onion

1/2 cup mayonnaise
3 tablespoons lemon juice
2 cups crisp shredded cabbage
2 cups crushed potato chips

Combine all ingredients with exception of cabbage and potato chips. Just before serving, stir in the crisp cabbage and crushed potato chips. Heap on a lettuce leaf, sprinkle top with crushed potato chips. Garnish with deviled egg or tomato wedges. This recipe can be doubled, tripled, whatever is needed, for company and club groups. The cabbage and potato chips extend the tuna fish in a remarkable manner. Makes 6 servings.

Honey Dressing

1/3 cup honey
1/3 cup catsup
1/4 teaspoon salt
1 teaspoon Worcestershire sauce

3/4 cup salad oil
3 tablespoons vinegar
juice of 1 small onion
2 tablespoons celery seeds

Combine ingredients in the order given, beating well. (To prepare onion juice, cut onion and scrape to release juice.) Serve on fruit or vegetable salads. Makes 1 1/2 cups.

Smashing Salad Dressing

2 cups real mayonnaise
2 cloves garlic, minced
2 tablespoons lemon juice
6 tablespoons Parmesan cheese

1/2 cup half-and-half or frozen
    nondairy creamer, thawed
salt and pepper to taste

Combine ingredients and beat with a fork or wire whisk until blended and mixture is light and fluffy. Chill several hours before using. Store unused portion in covered jar in refrigerator. This will keep up to a month if a nondairy creamer is used—the type found in the freezer section of the store. It is delicious with head lettuce, romaine lettuce, cauliflower, or a combination of fresh vegetables. Makes 3 cups.

Superb Chicken Salad

5 cups cooked cubed chicken
2 tablespoons oil
2 tablespoons orange juice
2 tablespoons vinegar
1/2 teaspoon salt
3 cups cooked rice
1 1/2 cups seedless grapes

1 1/2 cups sliced celery
1 13 1/2-ounce can pineapple
    chunks, drained
1 11-ounce can mandarin oranges,
    drained
1 cup toasted slivered almonds
1 1/2 cups mayonnaise

Combine chicken, oil, orange juice, vinegar, and salt. Refrigerate for at least 1 hour or longer, even overnight. Add remaining ingredients. Toss lightly. Serve in lettuce-lined bowl or in individual lettuce cups on salad plates. Makes 12 to 15 servings.

Macaroni Salad

1 8-ounce package macaroni
1/2 cup white vinegar
1/4 cup cider vinegar
1 cup water
1 1/2 cups sugar

1 tablespoon Accent (optional)
1 tablespoon parsley flakes
1 tablespoon prepared mustard
1 teaspoon garlic salt
vegetables of your choice

Use shell, bows, or any interestingly shaped macaroni. Cook macaroni according to directions. Drain. Combine dressing ingredients in a jar, cover, and shake well. Add vegetables to macaroni—cucumber slices, onion rings, cauliflower, radish slices, sliced celery, cooked green peas. Pour enough dressing over mixture to coat, toss, and refrigerate overnight. Remaining dressing will keep well refrigerated in a covered jar for another day. Makes 8 to 10 servings.

Three P Salad

1 cup drained cooked peas
1/2 cup chopped peanuts

1/4 cup chopped sweet pickles
mayonnaise or salad dressing

Combine ingredients with enough mayonnaise or salad dressing to moisten. Cubed cheddar cheese makes a nice addition to this salad, but then it wouldn't be called Three P Salad. Chill and serve in lettuce cups. Makes 4 servings.

14. The Telephone

~~~~~~

For those who lived in isolated, far-flung farmhouses of southwest Iowa in the middle of the twentieth century, the telephone was a vital link to the outside world. It gave farm families a line of communication with anyone, anywhere. Friends and family members were as close as a phone call.

Our Farragut telephone service was started in the early 1900s as a private company by a man named Jesse Whisler who strung a single line the seven miles between Farragut and the telephone office in the larger town of Shenandoah. It served only a few patrons. By 1904, nine men had joined Jesse to become members of a local telephone corporation. They set up a switchboard in the café in Farragut and, as they provided more lines to the homes in town, the number of customers increased. Eventually, they extended the wires to create party lines to the houses in the country.

Even with the advantages the telephone was bringing to the rural areas, some people objected to paying for the service or complained about having telephone poles erected close to their houses. The companies received permission to put their poles on public land along the roadside, and finally almost everyone recognized the value of this new-fangled contraption.

Because several families shared the same line, the early companies established rules for the use of the telephone to minimize problems. A customer could have the phone disconnected for refusing to pay an equal share of the expenses, or for using profanity, or for causing a disturbance on the line, or for singing or whistling (a rule no doubt due to the fact that in the early days of the telephone, people *did* sing and whistle over the lines). All conversations, including business, were to cease when someone put in a call for a doctor. Some telephone exchanges frowned upon unnecessary calls on Sunday, children meddling with the phone, and nonsense on the line. The rule that conversations be limited to five minutes except in the case of pressing business was never vigorously enforced, nor was the one which decreed that those listening in on someone else's call would have their phone use suspended.

When radio stations came into existence in the 1920s, farmers who owned both a radio and a telephone sometimes gave out a single long "general" ring which went to all the telephones on their line. When they heard enough clicks to know the neighbors were listening, they would put the mouthpiece of the phone near the radio speaker and let the listeners hear the program. Rules were made to eliminate this practice and, as more people purchased radios, the desire to share the exciting new form of communication and entertainment over the telephone ended.

By the 1940s, our local corporation had built a three-room gray-and-white cement block building on Farragut's main street to house the telephone office. One room held a boxy, battery-operated switchboard, and the other two rooms provided a home for the operator everyone called "Central."

Central would sit during the day in front of the switchboard that displayed all the numbers of the families and businesses of the Farragut company. When a call came in, a small metal flap flipped down to disclose a hole and a light. Central would pick up a plug fastened to a wire and push it into the hole in the switchboard, connecting her with the caller. "Number please," she'd say. Once she heard the number or the name of the person the caller wanted, Central would push a second plug into the appropriate hole to connect the two phones, then depress a button or lever to ring the needed phone. When the callers hung up their receivers, the switchboard lights went off, Central pulled the plugs, and the little metal flaps flipped up to cover the holes until the next call came in.

Central provided us with around-the-clock service, although it was understood that only emergency calls were to be made after 10:00 P.M. When she went to bed in the room adjoining the telephone equipment, Central would connect the switchboard to a bell that rang when someone called. It would awaken her, and she would get out of bed and hurry to connect the call.

Fern Carmichael was Central during some of the years we lived on the farm. I can remember lifting the receiver and turning the crank at the side of our telephone to send a signal to the switchboard. When she answered I'd say, "Fern, will you ring Fair Troxel?" Fern knew most of the local numbers by heart. She also knew where most of us were at any given time. If Fair did not answer, Fern could probably tell me where she was. "I saw her going into the grocery store. I'll ring and see if she's there." And soon Fair would be on the phone to take my message. If one of the country social clubs was meeting, Fern knew where the gathering was being held and who was in attendance. She would put any calls through to the meeting place instead of to our homes. She was, in effect, everyone's secretary.

Cottonwood Farm was on a party line that included fourteen families. When a call came through to any house on the line, all the phones rang at the same time, so each house had an identifying number of rings. Our ring was two shorts and a long. Some people lifted the receiver only to answer their own ring, but it was not unusual for individuals to pick up the phone and listen in on their neighbors' conversations. "Rubbering" was what some people called it when someone was listening on the party line.

A "general," or "line call," on country telephones was one long ring sounding simultaneously in all the houses connected by the same line. Everyone rushed to lift the receiver and hear whatever message Central was announcing over the wire. Several weeks after we moved to the farm, the long, insistent ring of a line call awakened me at midnight

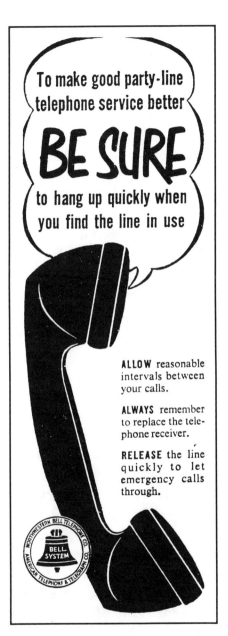

Ad in the October 20, 1952,
Shenandoah Evening Sentinel.

from a sound sleep. I groped my way to the living room and picked up the receiver to hear Fern say, "John Swisher's house is on fire. He needs help."

I shook Robert awake, helped collect clothing for him, held open the door, and watched as he drove down the lane. I could see other farmers' cars speeding past on their way to the Swisher farm. I very much wanted to go along but could not leave our sleeping children.

Robert returned several hours later, tired and dirty. "The fire started in the basement," he told me as we sat at the kitchen table drinking hot cocoa. "Farragut's volunteer fire department drove their truck out from town and used their pumping equipment while the rest of us started a bucket brigade. Smoke and water caused the most damage."

Robert took a sip of cocoa and wiped soot from his forehead. "John and Gladys were lucky they woke up and phoned in the alarm. That line call saved their house."

While Fern ran the switchboard for the phone company, Myrtle Brooks, who lived a mile north of us, was the unofficial communication center of our neighborhood party line. No matter whom a call was intended for, when the phone rang everyone knew that Myrtle would be listening. If someone rang our number and neither Robert nor I answered, Myrtle would come on the line, find out who the caller was, and, if it was someone she knew, she would tell the person where we were and when we would return.

Most of the families on our line considered Myrtle an important source of information about local activities. She was more up-to-date than the newspaper, more accurate than the radio newscasters, and more aware of the concerns and joys of the people on her telephone line than any other resident of the area. She listened not only to satisfy her own curiosity but also to share what she heard. If someone on our party line called to report a lost cow or a problem with farm machinery, Myrtle would pass the news along and the men would gather up their tools and go to help a fellow farmer repair broken machinery or find lost livestock. If someone in a household was sick and needed a doctor, minister, or, as happened on occasion, the undertaker, Myrtle sent word to the neighbors, and the women would head for their kitchens

Our good friend and neighbor Myrtle Brooks was the information hub for our telephone party line. Dale Brooks photo.

to stir up a casserole, mix up a cake, or bake a pie to take to the home of the friend in need.

Myrtle was a member of the same Friendly Fairview rural neighborhood club to which I belonged. Almost every time she entertained the members she would serve her banana cake. And whenever we had potluck dinners at the church, which was as often as anyone could conjure up a reason for one, Myrtle brought her banana cake. It was so delicate and tasty that every time I ate a piece, I would ask Myrtle to give me the recipe. "No!" she would say emphatically. "It's special. If I give you the recipe, you'll make it and get compliments, and it won't be mine any more!"

This went on for over two years until late one evening when our telephone rang. When I answered, a friend on the other end of the line said, "Evelyn, I want to make bread for company tomorrow, and I'd like the recipe you ran a couple of weeks ago in your 'Up a Country Lane' column for your multigrained bread. Can you give it to me over the phone?"

Myrtle's voice cut across the line. "Wait. Wait a minute, Evelyn," she said. "I don't have any clothes on. I was in the tub taking a bath when the phone rang, so I need to put on my robe and turn on the light so I can get something to write with. Will you wait?" My caller and I chatted until Myrtle came back on the party line and told us she was clothed, she had the light turned on, and, with pencil and paper in hand, she was ready to write.

The next morning Myrtle rang my number. "Evelyn," she said, "I want to thank you for waiting until I could take down that recipe last night. It isn't at all like the way I make bread, and it sure sounds good." Then, after a long pause and a deep breath, she concluded, "By the way, I've decided to give you my banana cake recipe. I'll bring it to church Sunday." Thanks to that call on our telephone party line, Myrtle's treasured cake recipe became mine.

Myrtle's Famous Banana Cake

1 3/4 cups sugar	1 teaspoon baking soda
1/2 cup butter	1 cup mashed bananas
2 eggs, beaten	2 1/4 cups sifted cake flour
1/2 cup buttermilk	1 teaspoon vanilla flavoring

Cream together the sugar and butter. (High-grade margarine can be substituted for the butter if you prefer, but that is something Myrtle would never do.) When mixture is light and fluffy, add the eggs and continue beating until smooth. Dissolve the baking soda in the buttermilk and stir into batter. Add bananas, cake flour, and flavoring. Mix well and pour into two greased and floured 8-inch pans or one 9-by-13-inch baking pan. Bake at 350 degrees for 30 to 45 minutes. When I make the flat cake, I fill 4 to 6 cupcakes as well, for this makes a generous amount of batter. The cupcakes take about 20 minutes to bake. Myrtle always frosted her cake with Brown Sugar Frosting. Makes about 20 servings.

BROWN SUGAR FROSTING

3 tablespoons brown sugar, packed
3 tablespoons butter
3 tablespoons cream

1 1/2 cups powdered sugar
1 teaspoon vanilla flavoring
dash of salt

Heat brown sugar, butter, and cream together over low heat, stirring, until well blended and sugar is dissolved. Remove from fire and stir in remaining ingredients, using enough powdered sugar to make of spreading consistency. When smooth and creamy, frost the cake.

Robert's After-the-Fire Cocoa

4 tablespoons cocoa
3 tablespoons sugar
dash of salt

1/3 cup hot water
4 cups milk
1 teaspoon vanilla flavoring

Combine cocoa, sugar, salt, and hot water in a saucepan. Bring to a boil, stirring, and simmer for 1 minute to blend. Add milk and flavoring and bring just to the boiling point (it will bubble around the edges). If desired, whip with egg beater or whisk and serve with a big fat marshmallow in each cup. Makes 4 cups.

Homemade Hot Chocolate Mix

2 cups dry powdered milk
1 cup powdered sugar
6 ounces powdered nondairy
    creamer

2 pounds instant cocoa mix
1/4 teaspoon salt

Combine ingredients, mix well, and store in airtight container. For a cup of hot chocolate, combine 3 tablespoons of mix, 1 cup of boiling water, and 1/4 teaspoon vanilla. This is a good mix to carry on camping trips. When the commercial cocoa mixes came on the market, I found them handy to use. This recipe makes them go farther so is more economical.

Bronzed French Toast

4 eggs
1/2 cup half-and-half
1/2 cup milk
1 teaspoon sugar

1/4 teaspoon nutmeg
1 teaspoon cinnamon
6 to 8 slices bread

Beat eggs with fork. Add half-and-half and milk. Stir in sugar and spices. Coat bread on each side in this egg mixture. Brown in a little butter or margarine in a skillet. Serve with hot syrup. Orange french toast can be made by substituting orange juice for part of the liquid and adding the grated rind of 1 orange. Combined with sausage or bacon, this makes for a substantial meal. Makes 4 to 6 servings.

Apple Pancake

2 tablespoons butter
1/3 cup sugar
1/2 teaspoon cinnamon
2 or 3 apples

3 tablespoons flour
3 egg yolks
3 tablespoons milk
3 egg whites

Melt butter in bottom of 8-inch skillet which can be put in oven (has metal handle or no handle). Stir sugar and cinnamon into butter. Peel and core apples and slice into 1/4-inch slices. Add to butter mixture. Cook over low heat 2 or 3 minutes. Combine flour, egg yolks, and milk and beat well. Beat egg whites until stiff and gently fold into egg yolk mixture. Pour batter over apple slices, spreading out to edge of pan. Bake in a 400-degree oven for 20 minutes. Turn out on serving platter, cut in wedges, and serve with syrup, fruit preserves, sour cream, or yogurt. Makes 4 servings.

Oatmeal Pancakes

1 1/2 cups rolled oats
2 cups buttermilk
2 eggs, beaten
2 tablespoons oil
3/4 cup flour

1 teaspoon sugar
1 teaspoon baking soda
1 teaspoon baking powder
dash of salt

Combine oats—either old-fashioned or quick—and buttermilk. Let stand about 5 minutes. Beat in eggs and oil. Combine dry ingredients and mix in just until combined. Fry on a hot griddle. Serve with syrup, fruit, or preserves. Makes about 12 pancakes, depending on size.

Your Own Maple Syrup

2 cups white sugar
2 cups brown sugar, packed
2 cups white corn syrup

2 cups water
2 teaspoons maple flavoring

Combine ingredients and cook, stirring, until sugars are dissolved and mixture boils. Simmer about 5 minutes. Serve hot on pancakes, waffles, or french toast. Store in covered jar in refrigerator. Makes 5 cups.

Potato Cakes

2 cups raw grated or cooked
   mashed potatoes
1 egg

2 tablespoons chopped onion
2 tablespoons flour
salt and pepper

Combine ingredients and shape into patties. Brown in a little shortening for a hearty addition to any meal of the day, but especially for breakfast. Makes 4 cakes.

Overnight Biscuits

2 cups flour
1 tablespoon sugar
4 teaspoons baking powder
1/2 teaspoon salt

1/2 cup shortening
1 egg, beaten
2/3 cup milk

Sift or stir flour, then blend with other dry ingredients. Cut in shortening until mixture resembles coarse crumbs. Combine liquid ingredients, beat with a fork. Add to dry mixture. Blend gently. Turn out on floured breadboard and knead gently about 20 times. Roll or pat dough 3/4 inch thick. Cut into 2-inch rounds. Place on ungreased baking sheet about 1 inch apart. Chill at least 1 hour. These can be refrigerated for several hours or overnight to have ready to pop into the oven in the morning for a delicious fresh hot bread—especially good to use for company breakfasts or brunches. Bake at 425 degrees about 12 minutes or until golden brown. Makes about 15 biscuits, depending on size.

15. Schools

~~~~~~~~~~~~~~~~~~~~~~~~~~~~~~~~~~

Disagreements existed among rural people just as they do any-where, but no situation created more anger across the farmland than when the little country schoolhouses closed and farm children were required to attend the consolidated schools in town. Even though there were no longer enough children to warrant having dozens of country schools and even though most people could see the educational advantages available in the town schools, giving up a cherished local school was difficult for everyone. Arguments over school consolidation could turn neighbor against neighbor with a divisiveness much deeper than any differences over politics or religion. Even after the boundaries of the new school districts had been drawn and the doors of the country schools closed for the last time, the pain of loss persisted for a very long time in the hearts of farm families.

It was not surprising that our neighbors, especially the descendants of the area's early settlers, were so defensive about their country schools. The pioneers had arrived with a great thirst for knowledge. They built country schoolhouses, at least one for each township, about four to six miles apart. The schools were attended by the settlers' children and then their grandchildren. Everyone used the buildings as community centers—for voting, literary societies, singing groups, box

The Fairview schoolhouse. Marjorie Hayes-Donaldson photo.

socials, and, until churches were built, Sunday school and worship services.

Each neighborhood imagined its school to be unique, but they were amazingly alike. Most were of wood frame construction. Children hung their coats on nails or hooks in an entrance hall just inside the front door. Beneath the coat hooks was a bench for lunch pails, a water pail, and a wash basin. The main room contained rows of well-used desks of varying sizes. The smallest desks for the littlest children were at the front of the room, the sizes graduating toward the largest seats at the back for the oldest students. Each desk had a shelf underneath for books, tablets, and pencils. Sometimes the teacher's desk stood on a raised platform in front of a large chalkboard. Most of the school buildings had no telephone and no running water. Heat came from a wood or coal stove in the middle of the room.

The only teacher at each school was usually a woman who had received her education through "normal training" classes in high school. After passing a county certification test, she could teach all eight grades of a country school without further education. As regulations became more stringent, teachers eventually needed at least two years of college courses in order to earn certification.

The director for each school district was a man chosen by the other men of the area. Sometimes the most prominent farmers simply took turns as director, while other districts had school boards composed of three or four men. These were positions of respect and authority, for the director and board set the budget, chose the books, hired the teacher, and approved of the place where she lived. Sometimes directors fired a teacher for such infractions as dancing, card playing, dating during the week, or missing church on Sunday.

Even in the earliest days, country schools carried students only through the eighth grade. Those who wanted more education would then enroll in the high school in a nearby town. Some farmers drove their children to the high school each day or had them walk. Many other rural students lived with town families during the week while they attended classes and worked at part-time jobs or assisted with housekeeping and the care of children to earn their room and board.

All this began to change as the 1930s came to a close. Families were having fewer children. The amount of land a farmer could till was increasing, and that meant fewer farm families living in each township. State laws required that a country school had to have an average attendance of at least six students throughout the 180-day school year. If attendance fell below that number, the school was closed and the children sent to schools in town.

Many farm families feared the city schools. The advantages were obvious, of course—larger facilities, fuller curricula, expanded library facilities, better-trained staff, improved recreational opportunities, and school buses that would transport the children from their homes to the schools. But the farmers liked having the country schools near their homes. They liked having a say in who would teach their children and how that teaching would be done. More than a few wanted to shield their youngsters from radical ideas and influences they might encounter in town.

When the country schools in our neighborhood were closed, the children were tossed off in several directions. Those from farms northeast of us began going to school in Shenandoah, while some to the

Dulcie Jean waves from the Farragut school yard where she attended kindergarten.

southeast attended classes in Northboro. The Hamburg School District was south and west of us, the Riverton district was north and west, and the Farragut district was to the north. Some farmers managed to have the school district lines redrawn to place their houses into districts more to their liking. Others paid taxes in one district and tuition in another in order to maintain their independence in selecting the school they wanted for their children.

Almost all of the one-room country schools in southwest Iowa were gone by mid-century. The last in our area was the Hillsdale school located in St. Paul's Lutheran Church parish. Hillsdale had enough students and local support to stay open until 1957, when the superintendent of the Farragut school district persuaded Hillsdale's popular teacher to bring her skills to the town school. Resistance to consolidating Hillsdale finally eased, and the pupils followed their teacher to Farragut. The magical, identifiable sense of the neighborhoods based on the rural school districts, the center of the universe for many, the fabric of rural life for a time, was gone.

By the time our daughter, Dulcie Jean, was ready to start kindergarten, Cottonwood Farm was in the Farragut School District. The three-story brick building was typical of the schools in many towns. There

*Silver, the family dog-of-the-moment, meets Bob as he steps off the
school bus.*

was a classroom for each grade and more space to accommodate the
high school. Students could use the gymnasium for sports and physical
education, and, on a stage at one end, they presented plays and musical
performances. Cooks prepared and served hot lunches at the school,
and it was a relief to me, along with many of the farm women, not to
have to plan and make lunches to send along with our children.

Forty-eight youngsters made up Dulcie Jean's all-day kindergarten
class, products of consolidation and of the baby boom that had begun
after World War II. Many of her classmates were her friends from
neighboring farms and the Friendly Fairview Club members' children.
She shared part of her hour-long bus ride each morning with her
cousin, Larry Lynn Bricker. The same age as Dulcie Jean, he had always
been one of her favorite companions. Dulcie Jean never complained
about the ride even though she sometimes mentioned the roughhous-

ing and teasing that were part of the experience. Some months after school began I learned that one of the older girls often asked our daughter to sit with her. It was a kindly gesture from one who could have let the younger farm girl fend for herself.

None of our children had the experience of attending a one-room school, but something they shared with those who did was coming home from school hungry. As they alighted from the bus each afternoon, I would put glasses of cold milk on the kitchen table. If I had time to bake, I would greet them with a plate of cookies hot from the oven. We would pull our chairs around the kitchen table, look over spelling papers and drawings from art class, and tell one another about the day's events.

After School Cookies

3 cups puffed rice
2 tablespoons peanut butter
3 tablespoons butter or margarine

1/4 pound marshmallows
milk chocolate candy bar

Heat puffed rice in baking pan in a 350-degree oven for about 5 minutes. Melt peanut butter, butter or margarine, and marshmallows in top of double boiler over hot water. Stir until smooth. Pour peanut butter mixture over hot cereal and stir until well coated. Press into paper-lined muffin tins and place 1 or 2 squares of the milk chocolate candy bar on top of each. Heat in the oven for just a minute if needed to melt chocolate slightly. Smooth over top with knife. Cool. These are great after school treats. Add a candle and they make delightful little birthday "cakes" for a child's party. Makes 8 to 10.

Buckeyes

1/2 pound peanut butter
1 1/2 pounds powdered sugar
1 cup margarine, softened

1/2 teaspoon vanilla flavoring
1 12-ounce package chocolate chips

Blend peanut butter, sugar, margarine, and flavoring. Shape into balls and place on cookie sheet and chill. Melt chocolate chips in top of double boiler over hot (not boiling) water. Hold balls with a toothpick and dip into chocolate on one side only. This makes them look like buckeyes, the large nutlike seed of the horse chestnut tree. Makes about 5 dozen.

Butterscotch Refrigerator Cookies

4 cups flour
1 teaspoon baking soda
1 teaspoon cream of tartar
1/4 teaspoon salt
1 cup brown sugar, packed

1 cup white sugar
1 cup butter or margarine
2 eggs
1 teaspoon vanilla flavoring
1 cup finely chopped nuts

Sift or stir dry ingredients together. Cream butter or margarine and eggs together and stir into dry mixture. Stir in flavoring and nuts. Add a little more flour if needed to handle well. When well mixed, shape into several rolls. Wrap in waxed paper or plastic wrap and chill. Slice 1/4 inch thick and place on greased cookie sheets. Bake at 350 degrees for 8 minutes or until lightly browned. This dough keeps nicely in the refrigerator for several days. It can also be wrapped in foil and frozen for longer storage. Makes 5 or 6 dozen crisp cookies.

No Roll Sugar Cookies

1 cup shortening
1 1/2 cups sugar
2 eggs
3 cups flour

2 teaspoons cream of tartar
1 teaspoon baking soda
dash of salt
1 teaspoon vanilla flavoring

Beat shortening, sugar, and eggs together until smooth and creamy. Add dry ingredients and flavoring. Roll into balls and dip into a mixture of 4 tablespoons sugar and 1 teaspoon cinnamon. Place on greased cookie sheet and press flat with a fork. Bake at 350 degrees for about 8 minutes or until light brown. Use multi-colored sugars instead of the cinnamon-sugar for a nice variation. Makes 4 to 5 dozen.

Cutout Sugar Cookies

1 cup butter or margarine
7/8 cup sugar
2 eggs
1 teaspoon vanilla flavoring

1/2 teaspoon almond flavoring
4 cups sifted flour (about)
1 teaspoon baking powder
1/2 cup cream or half-and-half

Cream butter or margarine and sugar. Beat in eggs and flavorings. Combine flour and baking powder and add alternately with cream or half-and-half. Chill. Add a little more flour if needed to handle well. Roll out to 1/4 inch thick and cut into shapes as desired. Place on greased cookie sheet and bake at 350 degrees for 8 to 10 minutes. Makes 5 dozen.

Snickerdoodles

1 cup butter or margarine
1 1/2 cups sugar
2 eggs
2 3/4 cups flour
2 teaspoons cream of tartar

1 teaspoon baking soda
1/4 teaspoon salt
1 teaspoon vanilla flavoring
1/4 teaspoon almond flavoring

Cream butter or margarine and sugar together. Beat in eggs. Sift dry ingredients together and stir into creamed mixture. Add flavorings. Chill dough. Roll into balls about the size of an English walnut. Dip into a mixture of 3 tablespoons sugar and 1 teaspoon cinnamon. Place on ungreased cookie sheet and bake at 375 degrees for about 8 to 10 minutes. These puff up at first and then flatten out and crinkle. Do not overbake; they should still be soft inside. Makes about 4 dozen.

Chewy Butterscotch Bars

1/2 cup butter or margarine
1 1/2 cups brown sugar, packed
2 eggs
1 1/2 cups flour

2 teaspoons baking powder
1 teaspoon vanilla flavoring
1 cup nuts

Melt butter or margarine and sugar together in saucepan. Bring to boil over low heat, stirring constantly. Cool slightly. Beat in eggs one at a time, beat well. Stir in remaining ingredients. Spoon into greased 9-by-13-inch baking pan. Bake at 350 degrees for 25 to 30 minutes. Cool and cut into bars. Makes 15.

Hale and Hearty Cookies

1 cup ground raisins
3/4 cup sugar
1/2 cup butter or margarine
1 egg or 2 egg whites

1/2 teaspoon almond flavoring
1 teaspoon baking powder
1 1/2 cups flour

Grind and measure raisins and set aside. Mix sugar and butter or margarine together until creamy. Stir in egg or egg whites and flavoring, then beat in dry ingredients gradually along with the ground raisins. Roll into balls and place on greased cookie sheet. Flatten with fork. Bake 8 to 10 minutes at 375 degrees. Makes about 2 dozen delightfully flavored, chewy cookies.

Kids' Chocolate Chip–Oatmeal Cookies

1 cup shortening
3/4 cup brown sugar, packed
3/4 cup white sugar
2 eggs, beaten
1 cup flour
1 teaspoon baking soda

1/4 teaspoon salt
1 teaspoon vanilla flavoring
2 cups rolled oats, toasted
1/2 cup nuts
1 6-ounce package chocolate chips
1/2 cup raisins or dates (optional)

Soften shortening to room temperature. (I like part margarine and part vegetable shortening.) Cream shortening and sugars together. Add beaten eggs. Beat well and stir in flour, baking soda, salt, and flavoring. Toast rolled oats in a skillet with 2 tablespoons butter, stirring constantly. Cool and add to batter. (I like the old-fashioned rolled oats, but quick oatmeal works fine also.) Mix in nuts and chocolate chips. Add raisins or dates if desired. Drop from a tablespoon on greased cookie sheet for large cookies, from a teaspoon for small. Press down a little to flatten. Bake at 375 degrees for 8 to 10 minutes or until light brown. Makes about 60 cookies, depending on size.

Pinwheel Cookies

1/2 cup butter or margarine
1/2 cup brown sugar, packed
1/2 cup white sugar
1 egg

1/2 teaspoon vanilla flavoring
2 cups flour
1/2 teaspoon baking soda
1/8 teaspoon salt

Cream butter or margarine, sugars, egg, and flavoring. Combine dry ingredients and blend in. Chill well. Divide dough into two portions and roll each into a 12-by-8-inch rectangle. Spread filling over the dough and roll up like a jelly roll. Wrap with waxed paper, plastic, or foil and chill. Slice and place on a greased cookie sheet and bake at 400 degrees for about 8 minutes. Makes 4 or 5 dozen.

DATE FILLING

1 pound pitted dates, chopped
1/2 cup brown sugar, packed

1/2 cup water
1/2 cup finely chopped walnuts

Combine dates, sugar, and water in a saucepan and cook, stirring constantly, until mixture boils and thickens. Cool. Add nuts and spread over cookie dough. Proceed as directed.

APRICOT FILLING

1 7-ounce package dried apricots,
   chopped
3/4 cup sugar

2 tablespoons lemon juice
3/4 cup pineapple juice
1 cup chopped pecans

Combine all ingredients except pecans and let stand 1 hour. Bring to a boil and cook, stirring, until thick. Cool. Add pecans. Spread on prepared dough and proceed as directed.

PINEAPPLE-CHERRY FILLING

1 cup undrained crushed pineapple
1/2 cup sugar

1/4 cup drained and diced
   maraschino cherries
1/2 cup nuts (optional)

Combine pineapple and sugar and cook until thick. Cool. Stir in cherries and nuts. Spread on dough and proceed as directed.

Walnut Frosties

1/2 cup butter or margarine
1 cup brown sugar, packed
1 egg
1 teaspoon vanilla flavoring

2 cups flour
1/2 teaspoon baking soda
1/4 teaspoon salt

Cream together the first four ingredients. Combine dry ingredients and stir into first mixture. Shape dough into 1-inch balls and put on ungreased cookie sheet. Make a depression in the center of each cookie and fill with Walnut Filling. Bake at 350 degrees for about 10 minutes or until lightly browned. Makes about 40 cookies.

WALNUT FILLING

1 cup chopped English walnuts
1/2 cup brown sugar, packed
1/4 cup sour cream

Combine and spoon a little into each depression in each cookie. Bake as directed.

16. A Country Church

~~~~~~

Houses of worship sprouted across the midwestern landscape in the middle and late 1800s just like Johnny Appleseed's orchards. The carriers of the seeds for these country churches were the circuit riders who, in their saddlebags, brought the early settlers the message of faith and hope when they deserved it and fear of damnation when they didn't.

In the countryside near Cottonwood Farm, three Methodist churches were organized about 1880, Locust Grove, Summit, and Madison. St. Paul's Lutheran Church, established in 1902 by several German settlers, stood in a field a few miles away. Catholic churches in the towns of Hamburg, Shenandoah, and Imogene served the needs of members of that faith. As settlers of other beliefs arrived in southwest Iowa, they established more churches like the Presbyterian, Mormon, Baptist, and Congregational. It was not unusual for people of different faiths to marry and join already established congregations.

Rural and small town churches gave farm families a sense of stability, of belonging, and of support when troubles came. They provided places where people of all ages could come to worship. Year-round Sunday schools and summer Bible schools gave the children instruction in religious subjects. The churches marked the passage of the year

Madison Methodist Church was located two miles south of Cottonwood Farm.
Madison church photo.

with holiday observances. Ministers and priests provided guidance in the lives of their parishioners by preaching sermons, performing their wedding ceremonies, baptizing their infants, burying their dead, and sometimes playing the organ, leading the choir, and sweeping the floor.

The churches were so much a foundation of farm life that I was surprised to discover that not everyone belonged. One of our neighbors told me he was not a member because he felt he could be just as devout a Christian on his tractor out in the fields as he could be sitting in a church pew. Another thought he lived a more exemplary life than the people who did attend services, so he didn't need to go. Even so, when nonmembers needed the support of the church communities, the doors were always open.

We attended the Madison Methodist Church. In 1880, a Methodist circuit rider passing through southwest Iowa held a revival meeting in a nearby country schoolhouse. He sufficiently impressed nine people to form a Methodist Episcopal congregation. Another revival meeting in 1883 persuaded more people to join, and by 1885 the congregation

The small foyer at the rear of the church sanctuary was a fine place to visit with the minister and friends following the service. Ralph Miller photo.

was large enough to erect a white frame church. The total cost of the building was $1,500, with $500 still due on the day the building was dedicated. At the dedication service, as the choir sang a rousing rendition of "Hold the Fort," the minister passed his hat, and those in attendance put in enough money to pay off the debt.

Madison's architecture was much like that of the other small churches across the farmland. It was rectangular in shape and topped by a simple bell tower which was too low and too blunt to be called a steeple. Around the church stood a grove of tall elm trees. Near the fence that divided the churchyard from a cornfield stood two outhouses, one for men and boys, the other for women and girls. An outdoor pump provided the church building's only water.

Three cement steps led up to a wide platform set in front of double front doors. Inside the front door was a small foyer where the parishioners shucked off their coats and hung them on hooks along the wall. During stormy weather they put their snowy or muddy boots and closed umbrellas on newspapers on the floor. The entryway had another use as well. It was just large enough to hold a coffin while the mourners passed by at the close of a funeral service.

The interior of the Madison church was modest. Early Methodists believed in unpretentious decor, partly from the theology of simplicity and partly from their lack of money. The windows, with a gentle nod toward more elegant designs, were gracefully arched. The glass was lightly frosted at the bottom, but the top portion was clear and provided a view of trees and sky as inspiring to the worshipers as any stained glass might have supplied. Pews were located on each side of a central aisle that led up to the front of the room and a slightly raised platform with a sturdy wooden pulpit located in the center. A large square metal grille embedded in the floor in front of the pulpit allowed the heat to come directly into the main room of the building from a pipeless, coal-fired furnace. During worship services on especially cold winter days, the people would gather on the front pews close to the heat. The rest of the time they sat in the seats near the back of the church, as members in most congregations are prone to do.

During the time we attended, the Madison church folks decided to build and install a central wooden altar at the front of the church, hang an ornamental cloth, known as a dossal drape, behind it, and paint the woodwork around the front windows. Soon every one of the thirty families who made up Madison's membership was busy putting forth ideas and raising money to pay for the undertaking. Following the time-tested patterns of the other churches in the area when they needed to raise extra funds, the women donated food and cooked chicken dinners with all the trimmings and invited the public to come eat and leave a freewill offering to enrich the coffers. They held a rummage sale in the churchyard and organized bake sales, bazaars, and box socials. They had a splendid time until they needed to decide which colors to use on the new project.

"It takes a lot of give and take just to choose the color of the dossal drape, let alone make the rest of the decisions," sighed the Sunday school superintendent after one stressful discussion. "Some have to give and some have to take." It did seem strange that so much tension developed over such an insignificant choice.

As a minister's daughter and a worker in churches in the different areas where I had lived through the years, I was aware that such petty

The newly remodeled sanctuary at Madison church decorated for Christmas. Kenneth Smalley photo.

disagreements were universal. I tried to understand why the easier the problem the harder it can be to resolve. I finally concluded that every person involved feels he or she has the right answer to a quandary, which makes it almost impossible to consider that someone else might have a better idea. Working through the simple arguments also gives the members a way to act out some of the aggravations they generally push into their subconscious, since most people behave civilly to each other in the rest of their interactions. I eventually came to realize that such situations also reflect who has the authority in an organization. The Madison difficulties were typical; they were not really about the color of paint or the fabric for the dossal curtain but about who was in control and who had the power to make the decisions.

Once the volunteers painted the woodwork, built and installed the new altar, and hung the drapes, tempers calmed, friendships were restored, and almost everyone agreed that the interior of the church looked wonderful.

If the circuit-riding preacher who started the church had walked into the Madison sanctuary the Sunday following the completion of the project, he would surely have been surprised and delighted to see what

The youth choir at Madison church was a wonderful mixture of ages (from five-year-old Dulcie Jean, front-right, to high school students). At left is accompanist Leta Smalley.

his efforts had created. Enthusiastic people filled the room, right up to and including the front pew. The youth choir sang heartily and the minister preached a rousing dedication sermon, then everyone went downstairs and enjoyed a bountiful potluck dinner.

Church Dinner Cabbage Slaw

1 tablespoon unflavored gelatin
1/4 cup cold water
1 cup white vinegar
1 1/2 cups sugar
1/4 cup water
1 teaspoon salt
1 teaspoon celery salt

1/2 teaspoon black pepper
1 cup salad oil
8 to 10 cups shredded cabbage
1 medium onion, minced
1 green pepper, diced
2 large carrots, grated

Dissolve gelatin in cold water. Heat vinegar, sugar, and 1/4 cup water together. When this is boiling, remove from heat and stir in dissolved gelatin mixture and the seasonings. Cool. Gradually beat in oil. Combine dressing with prepared vegetables. Chill several hours or up to

24 hours before serving; the gelatin is not enough to set the salad firm, just enough to keep it crisp. This dressing keeps well in a covered glass jar in the refrigerator. Makes 15 to 20 servings.

Communion Bread

1/2 cup butter
1/3 cup sugar
2 1/4 cups flour
1/2 teaspoon salt

1/4 teaspoon baking powder
1/2 cup milk
1 egg white, beaten

Cream butter and sugar. Add dry ingredients alternately with milk. Fold in stiffly beaten egg white. Pat dough onto a greased and floured 11-by-17-inch jelly roll pan. Bake at 350 degrees for about 20 to 30 minutes. Do not brown. Cut into 1/2-inch cubes. Serves about 50.

Baked Butter Beans

2 15-ounce cans butter beans
1/2 cup brown sugar, packed
1/2 cup half-and-half

1/2 cup catsup
3 slices bacon, diced
1/4 cup finely chopped onion

Drain one can of butter beans, but include the juice from the second. Combine ingredients and bake at 350 degrees until it thickens. Very good cooked with sliced rounds of wieners.

Macaroni and Cheese

1 pound elbow macaroni
1 small onion, diced
1/4 cup butter
3 tablespoons flour
1 cup milk
1 cup half-and-half

1 tablespoon Worcestershire sauce
1/2 teaspoon dry mustard
salt and pepper to taste
1/2 pound grated medium or sharp
    cheddar cheese
3/4 cup buttered bread crumbs

Cook macaroni according to directions. Drain and put in casserole. Stir in onion. Stir and melt butter and flour together until bubbly, gradually add milk and half-and-half, and continue cooking over low heat, stirring, until mixture thickens. Add Worcestershire sauce, mustard, and salt and pepper. Remove from heat and stir in cheese and continue stirring as cheese melts and mixture is creamy. Pour over macaroni in casserole. Top with buttered bread crumbs. Bake at 350 degrees for 30 minutes or until nicely brown on top. Makes 12 to 15 servings.

Baked Beans with Dates

1 pound 5 ounce–can pork and
   beans with tomato sauce
1 tablespoon brown sugar, packed
1 tablespoon molasses

1 cup finely chopped dates
4 slices bacon, diced
1 small onion

Combine all ingredients except onion in 1-quart casserole or bean pot. Peel 1 small onion and bury it in the beans. Cover and bake for 30 minutes at 350 degrees. Remove cover and bake for 30 more minutes. Remove onion and serve. This can be put together the day before you want to use it and refrigerated until time to bake. Makes 6 to 8 servings.

Hearty Bean Casserole

1 15-ounce can yellow butter beans
1 15-ounce can kidney beans
1 16-ounce can pork and beans
1/2 cup brown sugar, packed
1/2 cup catsup

salt and pepper
1 small onion, chopped
1 pound hamburger, browned
1 tablespoon prepared mustard
2 tablespoons vinegar

Combine ingredients and bake at 325 degrees for 1 hour. A fine large casserole for covered-dish dinners.

Eggplant Casserole

1 medium or large eggplant	1 cup canned or cooked tomatoes
3/4 cup grated sharp cheese	1 cup whole kernel corn
1 small or medium onion, chopped	1 4-ounce can mushroom, stems
1/2 green pepper, chopped	and pieces, drained
2 eggs, well beaten	1 cup dry bread crumbs
2 tablespoons butter, melted	

Wash, peel, and dice eggplant. Cook in salted boiling water for 10 minutes or until just barely tender. Remove from fire; drain. Add cheese to hot eggplant and stir gently until melted. Stir in remaining ingredients. Salt and pepper to taste. Spoon into casserole and top with bread crumbs. Bake at 350 degrees for 30 minutes. Makes 6 to 8 servings.

Potluck Chicken with Dressing

1 stewing chicken	1/2 teaspoon sage
1/3 cup butter or margarine	1/2 teaspoon parsley
2/3 cup flour	1/2 teaspoon salt
4 cups chicken broth	1 tablespoon poultry seasoning
1 1-pound loaf bread, cubed	hot water or broth to moisten
3 to 4 tablespoons chopped onion	5 or 6 eggs, slightly beaten
1 bunch celery, chopped	1/4 cup bread crumbs
1/2 teaspoon celery salt	2 tablespoons butter or margarine,
1/2 teaspoon pepper	melted

Cover the chicken with water and boil until meat is tender. (A pressure pan brought to 10 pounds pressure will cook a chicken nicely in 20 minutes.) Cool. Reserve broth. Remove meat from bone, discard bones, and cut meat into bite-sized pieces. Melt butter or margarine in a large skillet or heavy pan. Stir in flour and continue stirring until mixture is smooth and bubbly. Gradually stir in chicken broth. Continue cooking and stirring until mixture thickens into gravy. Remove from fire and cool to lukewarm. Meanwhile, make a dressing by combining bread cubes, onion, celery, and seasonings. Add enough hot water or hot broth to moisten mixture. Grease a large baking dish or casserole—9 by 13 inches or larger—and put chicken in an even layer over the bottom. Pat the dressing over the top of the chicken. Beat the eggs lightly and blend into the lukewarm gravy mixture. Season with salt if desired. Spoon over top of dressing. Top with bread crumbs coated with the melted butter or margarine. Bake at 375 degrees for 1 hour or until custardlike mixture is set. Cut into squares to serve. Makes 20 servings.

Unusual Fruit Cobbler

1/2 cup butter or margarine
1 cup flour
1 cup sugar
1 teaspoon baking powder
1/4 teaspoon salt

1 cup milk
1/2 teaspoon vanilla flavoring
2 cups fruit (fresh or canned, drained)

Melt butter or margarine in casserole or 8-by-8-inch baking dish. Sift dry ingredients together. Combine milk and vanilla and stir into dry mixture. Pour this batter over the melted butter but *do not stir!* Spoon the fruit over the batter. Bake at 350 degrees for 30 to 40 minutes or until batter covers the fruit and browns on top. Wonderful served warm with ice cream or whipped cream. Peaches, apples, cherries, blueberries, pineapple—any fruit is excellent! Serves 6 to 8.

Fruit Chef's Salad

1 small head of lettuce, pulled into bite-sized pieces
1 cup cottage cheese
1 cup pineapple chunks, drained

1 unpeeled apple, diced
1/4 cup chopped English walnuts
1/4 cup raisins
3 tablespoons french dressing

Combine ingredients with enough dressing to moisten. Serve in a pretty bowl or as individual salads in lettuce cups. Garnish with orange segments. This simple lettuce and fruit salad can be varied with different seasonal fruits. It makes a fine dinner salad. When served as refreshments, add crispy crackers for a nice accompaniment. Makes about 15 servings, depending on amount of lettuce used.

17. Holidays

~~~~~~~~~~~~~~~~~~~~~~~~~~~

Every season on the farm was busy, and sometimes holidays went by almost unnoticed. But Thanksgiving, Christmas, Easter, Memorial Day, and the Fourth of July were events special enough for country folks to set aside some time from their labors for pleasure without feeling guilty.

Habits of frugality, started by their pioneer ancestors and continued through the years of the Great Depression and World War II, meant that many of the families in our neighborhood held simple, inexpensive celebrations. For those of us who were renting farms and had small incomes, that translated into "homemade." Robert used his carpentry tools and I plugged in my sewing machine, and we created most of our holiday decorations and gifts. We used the foods from our root cellar and meat locker for festive meals, including Christmas.

Robert taught a Sunday school class of four-year-olds for several years. One December, he coached them to approach the front of the sanctuary and act out the events of the first Christmas. A tiny Mary and Joseph dressed in bathrobes and towel headpieces walked up to a make-believe inn and knocked on the make-believe door.

"Come in," said the little boy who was acting the part of the innkeeper.

Robert was sitting on the front pew. He leaned toward his young

The Birkby family in December 1950.

innkeeper and whispered, "There was no room for Mary and Joseph. When they knock again, tell them to go away."

Joseph rapped on the door a second time. "Come in," said the young innkeeper.

"No! No!" Robert insisted. "You don't have any room for them."

"Oh, yes I do," the four-year-old answered firmly. "*I made room!*"

In the same way, farm families made room for Christmas. They cut cedar trees out of their timber and placed them near the altars of their churches. The decorating committees hung lights and silvery icicles from the branches. Candles on the window sills glowed into the darkness to show people the way as they drove up the roads and into the churchyards.

Christmas Eve programs seldom varied from church to church or from one year to the next. The children recited poems and sang "Jingle Bells" and "Away in the Manger." They presented plays about the meaning of Christmas, and the ministers offered prayers. The congregations sang "Silent Night" and "Joy to the World" as the spirit of love and anticipation filled the hearts of those in the small sanctuaries. The

A quiet moment following a holiday dinner. Left to right: Bob, Grandma Corrie, Lucretia Birkby, Dulcie Jean, and the children's great grandmother, Erie Birkby.

Sunday school teachers handed out sacks that usually held such treats as an apple, several pieces of brightly colored hard ribbon candy, and a chocolate or two with a firm vanilla center. Then it was time for the noisy children to lead the way out the doors and home to snuggle in their beds and dream of Christmas morning and the coming of Santa.

New Year's Eve, Lincoln and Washington's birthdays, Valentine's Day, and St. Patrick's Day all went by without much fuss. At Cottonwood Farm I made a cherry pie or two. The children helped me make cutout cookies, trimmed red hearts with lace, and turned green construction paper into shamrocks.

The next really important holiday of the year was Easter. Country children whose mothers raised laying hens had the advantage of a generous source of eggs for their Easter fun. The older boys and girls used darning needles to prick holes in the ends of the shells and helped their younger siblings blow the contents out of the shells and into a bowl to become scrambled eggs or omelets for supper. Next, they rinsed the shells with water and let them air dry. They dropped tablets of dye into glasses filled with water and then soaked the empty shells in the solutions until they turned pretty colors. They decorated the

Bob and his brother, Craig, show off their Easter egg tree.

colored eggs with decals or poster paints, then piled them in bowls on the tables or strung pieces of ribbon and yarn through the holes and hung them on Easter egg trees.

On Easter Sunday morning, the children hurried outdoors to find bunny nests filled with candy eggs. The Easter rabbit passing through our yard left goodies near the windmill, beside the sandbox, and under the back steps. But if the day was stormy, that bunny somehow found her way inside the house to tuck her nests near the stove, under the kitchen table, and behind the toy chest.

Easter morning church service was at the center of the celebration for most rural mid-Americans. People who never attended services any other week of the year put on their best clothes and drove to the church of their choice. They were met by gracious handshakes from the regular attendees, glorious music from the choir, abundant numbers of white lilies, and a message of hope from the minister. The remainder of the day was spent visiting and feasting with friends and relatives.

Dulcie Jean in her choir robe at Madison church on Easter Sunday.

Eating dinner in a restaurant in one of the nearby towns was an option for people who did not have anyone with whom to share or for those who preferred to have someone else do the cooking.

At the end of May came what we called Decoration Day, now known as Memorial Day. For midwestern families, it was more than a commemoration of wars past. It was also a time when families remembered all their departed forebears. It was, as my mother-in-law Lucretia said, a time to be with the relatives, even those who were no longer around.

Each Memorial Day our family went to the local cemeteries to decorate the graves with flowers picked from our gardens—peonies, iris, roses, marigolds—and sometimes dainty wild daisies from the creek bank. For containers we used water-filled mason jars or coffee cans covered with foil.

Local organizations held services in the cemeteries. The years following World War II brought out deep emotions in the participants as a teacher or minister shared a patriotic message, a high school quartet sang "The Battle Hymn of the Republic," the American Legion Post bugler sounded taps, and the firing squad shot off volleys from their rifles. Little boys rushed out as the service ended to gather up the spent shells from the grass—souvenirs of a day whose meaning they did not yet fully comprehend.

Memorial Day was also a history lesson for us. As grandparents, cousins, aunts, uncles, and parents walked together among the tombstones, the children listened while the adults reminded them who their ancestors were. "Now this is your great-great grandfather, Henry J. Carter," Lucretia Birkby would tell her grandchildren as she pointed to an aging marker. "He fought for the North in the Civil War and was captured by the South and went to Andersonville Prison in Georgia."

"This is your great-great grandfather Thomas Birkby's grave," Robert's father would tell the children. "In 1864 he traveled up the Missouri River with his wife, Mary Courtney. They got off the boat in Hamburg and started along the bluff road in a stagecoach. I've been told that when the driver stopped to rest his horses, Thomas climbed up one of the hills and picked out the land on the flat river bottom where he wanted to settle. He bought it with his life savings, a $1,000 bill he had secretly carried all the way from Illinois with him."

Bob and his Grandma Corrie place a basket of flowers on Grandpa Corrie's grave in Shenandoah.

We always stopped by my father's grave so that my mother could tell the youngsters how he had traveled in a covered wagon in 1886 with his parents and brothers and sister from Illinois to settle on a farm in central Kansas. This was oral tradition at its best, the passing of family history from the older adults to the children.

If Memorial Day was a time of thoughtfulness, the Fourth of July on the farm was full of fun. There were plenty of community celebrations with patriotic speeches, picnics, band concerts, and softball games in the parks. The country folks drove into town and joined in the festivities whenever they could, but if the hay was down, or cornfields still needed to be laid by, or animals required special attention, the farm families might be too busy to enjoy a full day of leisure. If nothing else, they could have a yard picnic.

We had such a picnic one busy Fourth of July at Cottonwood Farm.

Robert and I finished the farm work by the middle of the afternoon and set card tables out under the trees in the yard. His parents, Lucretia and Lawrence, arrived with potato salad coated with homemade dressing. My sister, Ruth Bricker, and her family brought tender, early sweet corn and loaves of delicious date bread. Robert's sister, Ruthella Barnard, her husband, Bob, and their children came bringing apple salad and watermelon. My mother walked into the yard carrying one of her elegant angel food cakes. By the time I added crunchy fried chicken, crisp green lime pickles, hot homemade rolls, freshly churned butter, and red strawberry jam, the tables fairly groaned.

A Fourth of July without homemade ice cream was as unthinkable on many farms as Christmas without presents. After we had eaten everything else, Robert got the hand-cranked freezer from the woodshed. I brought out the custard I had prepared earlier with some of our own thick country cream, fresh eggs, sugar, and vanilla flavoring, and poured it into the metal freezer can. With the lid firmly in place, Robert slid the can into the wooden bucket, scooped crushed ice and rock salt around the can, and fastened the crank on top of the freezer.

It took about thirty minutes of cranking with everyone taking a turn who expected to eat any of the dessert. The children started, but as the ice cream hardened, the women and men took over. When the ice cream was frozen so hard the paddles would no longer turn, Robert lifted the dasher out of the container and put it in one of our large dishpans. Each child had a spoon ready, for licking the paddles was one of the glorious delights of helping crank homemade ice cream. That done, Robert filled soup bowls with the delicious treat and passed them around.

The other families among our guests had no cows to milk, but Robert did, so as dusk gradually crept over the farm, he led a gaggle of giggling kids to the pasture to bring in the cows.

Once the milking was done, the men sat together at one side of the yard and discussed the weather, the growing crops, the health of their livestock, and politics. A few puffed on cigars. They did not light up often, but a number of the men in our vicinity did so on holidays. Smoking a cigar at the conclusion of a Sunday meal, during trips to the Masonic lodge meetings in town, as they trucked livestock to the market in Omaha, or on holidays, was one way they marked the specialness of an event.

The women liked to sit and visit on the porch away from the mosquitoes and flies. Our conversation usually centered around the health of our families, the state of our gardens, how many jars of jam were in our cellars, a couple who were having marital problems, and the arrival of a new minister and his family at the Farragut-Madison parish.

After dark, we brought out fireworks. The children lit tiny black buttons and gleefully greeted the fiery "snakes" that crawled out. Robert touched off several small skyrockets that trailed smoke as the tubes zoomed upward and exploded in brilliant red-and-gold sparks. He fastened whirligigs onto the trunk of a cottonwood tree where they turned and twirled and sent out fiery red-and-green circles. The youngsters hopped around the yard yelling as they waved glowing sparklers over their heads.

By the time the sparklers had burned out, the fireflies were flashing their courtship messages from the bushes along the yard fence. As the elders sat, satiated and weary, the cousins ran and shouted in a final burst of energy as they caught some of the tiny lightning bugs and put them in glass jars with air holes punched in the lids. At last the youngsters sat quietly watching the twinkling glowworms inside the jars until their parents were ready to leave for home, then they unscrewed the lids and watched the tiny shimmering lights disappear into the soft dark of the warm summer night.

Robert's Favorite Homemade Ice Cream

2 1/4 cups sugar
1/3 cup flour
1/4 teaspoon salt
5 cups milk, scalded

6 eggs, beaten
1 quart half-and-half or whipping
  cream
1 to 2 tablespoons vanilla flavoring

Combine sugar, flour, and salt in a saucepan. Add scalded milk and cook over medium heat, stirring, until thick. Stir a little of this custard mixture into the beaten eggs, then return all to the hot mixture and cook another minute. Remove from heat and cool. Combine half-and-half or whipping cream and flavoring and stir into cooked mixture. Pour into a 1-gallon freezer can, put lid on, and fasten the crank in place. Put ice and rock salt around the freezer can. Turn the crank until the mixture is frozen, replenishing the ice and salt as needed. This can also be made with an electric ice cream freezer. Makes 32 half-cup servings, but no one wants to stop there, so plan on serving about 16.

Grandma Corrie's Angel Food Cake

12 egg whites
2 teaspoons cream of tartar
1 1/4 cups granulated sugar

3/4 teaspoon vanilla flavoring
1/4 teaspoon almond flavoring
1 cup sifted cake flour

Beat egg whites until foamy. Add cream of tartar. Continue beating and, as peaks begin to form, gradually beat in the sugar and flavorings. When soft peaks form, fold in cake flour which has been sifted before measuring and then sifted two more times. Pour batter into ungreased angel food cake pan. Bake in a 275-degree oven for 30 minutes then at 325 degrees for 30 more minutes. The cake should be golden brown on top and still have a glistening look which shows that it is still moist and not dry. Remove pan from oven and turn upside down, resting it on three cups, or place the center over the stem of a bottle so the angel food will cool upside down.

Ruth's Date Nut Bread

2 cups dates
1 1/2 cups boiling water
2 cups sugar
2 3/4 cups flour
2 teaspoons baking soda
1/4 teaspoon salt

1 tablespoon vegetable shortening
1 tablespoon vanilla flavoring
1 egg
1/2 to 3/4 cup English walnuts or
    pecans, chopped

Combine dates and boiling water; set aside. Combine remaining ingredients in a mixing bowl and add date mixture, liquid and all. Beat well. Spoon into a greased regular-sized bread pan (or two 3-by-7-inch bread pans). Bake at 350 degrees, 1 hour for the large loaf or 40 to 45 minutes for the small ones. Test for doneness—not doughy in middle—but do not overcook. This falls just a little as it cools, but that does not hurt the delicious flavor and texture of the loaf. It freezes well and is nice to use for gifts or to keep on hand for unexpected company. Makes 1 large loaf or 3 small ones.

Ruthella's Apple Salad

4 unpeeled red apples, diced
1/2 cup miniature marshmallows
1/4 cup chopped nuts (black
  walnuts preferred)

1 cup sliced and seeded red grapes
1/4 cup mayonnaise
1/4 cup cream, whipped, or 1/2 cup
  whipped topping

Combine first four ingredients in a bowl. Mix mayonnaise and whipped cream or whipped topping and fold in. The ingredients can be varied according to availability and preference. Makes 8 to 10 servings.

Lucretia's Potato Salad

6 boiled potatoes, peeled and diced
1 small onion, diced
1/4 cup chopped sweet pickles
1 tablespoon sugar
4 hard-cooked eggs, diced

salt and pepper to taste
1/4 cup mayonnaise or salad
  dressing
1/4 cup whipped topping

Any cooked potatoes can be used for potato salad, but Lucretia liked to boil small potatoes with their skins on, peel them while they were still warm, and then dice them into a bowl. Add remaining ingredients, first combining the salad dressing and whipped topping, or use Homemade Salad Dressing. For many years, Robert's mother made her own homemade dressing. Later, when good quality mayonnaise and salad dressings came on the market, she substituted those with an equal amount of whipped topping mixed in. It took her family a long time to discover that she had switched! Makes about 8 servings.

Homemade Salad Dressing

3 tablespoons sugar	6 tablespoons water
1 teaspoon dry mustard	6 tablespoons cider vinegar
1/4 teaspoon salt	4 eggs, beaten

Combine ingredients and cook in top of double boiler or over low heat, stirring constantly, until mixture coats a spoon. Dressing thickens as it cools. Spoon into jar, cover, and refrigerate until time to serve (it keeps well). When ready to serve, add a little cream or sour cream and more sugar if desired. Good on fruit and vegetable salads but especially nice on potato salad.

Easter Ham or Pork Chops with Cherries

1 3-pound cooked ham or 8 pork chops	1/4 teaspoon cinnamon
1 can sour cherries, drained	1/2 lemon, thinly sliced
1 tablespoon cornstarch	2 tablespoons honey
	1 tablespoon butter, melted

Blend cornstarch into cherry juice. Combine with remaining ingredients and cook over low heat, stirring, until clear and thick. Pour over cooked ham slices or cooked pork chops. Another method of cooking would be to spoon the sauce over ham or unbaked pork chops and bake in a 350-degree oven until meat is done.

New Year's Eve Pizza

1 package yeast
1 cup lukewarm water
1 teaspoon sugar
1 teaspoon salt

1 tablespoon olive oil
1 egg, beaten
3 1/2 cups flour

Stir yeast into 1/4 cup lukewarm water. Add sugar and let dissolve. In a bowl combine the rest of the water, salt, olive oil, and egg. Stir in the yeast mixture. Add enough flour to make a dough which can be kneaded. Knead well. Put in greased bowl and cover with a damp towel. Let rise until double. Punch down and refrigerate while you prepare the topping. Remove dough from refrigerator and cut into two parts. Pat each part into a pizza pan, stretching and spreading to cover. Fill and bake immediately. Bake at 425 degrees for 15 to 20 minutes. Makes 2 large pizzas.

PIZZA FILLING

1 1/2 pounds ground beef
1/2 cup chopped onion
1 to 2 tablespoons olive oil
1 4-ounce can mushrooms, stems
    and pieces, drained
1 6-ounce can tomato paste
1 8-ounce can tomato sauce

1/2 teaspoon garlic salt
1/2 teaspoon oregano
1/4 teaspoon pepper
salt to taste
1/2 pound mozzarella cheese
Parmesan cheese

Brown ground beef and onion in olive oil. Drain off excess fat. Stir in mushrooms, tomato paste, tomato sauce, and seasonings. Remove from fire. Put slices of mozzarella cheese over dough in pizza pans. Spoon half the meat mixture into each pan, covering the cheese. Sprinkle Parmesan cheese over the top. Other meats can be used besides the one given. Freezes well unbaked, tightly wrapped in freezer plastic wrap. Bake, unthawed, until done.

Holiday Cranberry Salad

1 pound cranberries
6 unpeeled apples
1 or 2 unpeeled oranges

1 cup sugar
1/2 cup chopped pecans

Wash cranberries. Pick out any unusable cranberries and discard. Wash and core apples and oranges. Grind all the fruits together. Stir in sugar and nuts. Chill, covered, for several hours or overnight. This will keep for a week or more. Excellent as a meat accompaniment. Makes about 8 to 10 servings.

Gooey Date Pudding

1 cup flour
1 teaspoon baking powder
1 cup brown sugar, packed
1 cup chopped dates
1/4 to 1/2 cup nuts

dash of salt
1/2 cup milk
1 cup brown sugar, packed
2 cups water
2 tablespoons butter or margarine

Mix first six ingredients in a bowl. Stir in milk. Spoon into an 8-by-8-inch greased baking dish. Combine remaining ingredients and bring to a boil. Spoon over the batter in the pan. Bake at 325 degrees for 45 to 50 minutes. The long, slow baking makes the boiled mixture thicken and become a delicious gooey bottom, and the cakelike date mixture rises to the top. Serves about 10.

Uncooked Fruit Cake

1 pound pitted dates
1 pound marshmallows
1 pound orange gumdrop candies
1 cup chopped nuts

1/2 cup sugar
1/2 cup cream, whipped, or 1 cup
    whipped topping
1 pound graham crackers

Cut dates, marshmallows, and orange gumdrops fine with scissors. Add nuts, sugar, and whipped cream or whipped topping. Roll graham crackers into crumbs and stir in. Form into a roll and wrap in waxed paper and refrigerate until time to slice and serve. Can be served like a cookie or on a plate with a dollop of whipped cream and a maraschino cherry on top. Makes about 20 servings, depending on thickness.

Ice Cream Sandwich

4 cups rice crispy cereal, crushed
1 cup coconut
1 cup chopped pecans

1 cup brown sugar, packed
1 cup butter or margarine, melted

Combine ingredients and sprinkle half in bottom of a 9-by-13-inch pan. Cut ice cream in slices about 1 inch thick and cover crumbs. Any kind of ice cream is fine, strawberry and Neapolitan are my favorites. Sprinkle remaining crumbs on top and freeze. Keep covered for long-time storage. Cut into squares. Great to make ahead for any festive gathering. Makes 12 to 15 squares.

18. Saturday Night in Town

~~~~~~

The winds of change moved across the country after the war. Better roads, more automobiles in the marketplace, and the availability of inexpensive gasoline made transportation more practical, and people began to travel longer distances for their shopping and entertainment. The grocery chains and the multi-store areas were already beginning to evolve, and, as the shopping centers grew and stayed open on Sundays, the era of Saturday night trips to town came to a close for rural Mid-Americans.

But the end came gradually. Even in the 1950s, a Saturday night in town was still one of the most exciting times of the week for those who lived in the country. In the horse-and-buggy days, the time and distance involved allowed farm families only one trip to town a week, and most of them chose Saturday. Those of us who continued to work in lonely settings in rural Iowa delighted in the same opportunity to get away from the farm, do errands in preparation for the week to come, and visit with other families. Rural children and teenagers enjoyed the time spent with others their own age.

On Saturday afternoon, the family got ready to go to town. The husband would do his chores and load the car or pickup with the eggs and cream he planned to sell. Then he would wash up and put on clean clothes. If the farmhouse had no bathroom, he might wait until

Farragut's main street about 1950. Alma Bickett Roland photo.

he got to town, then use the bath facilities at the local barbershop. Throughout the afternoon his wife did her tasks and prepared a hasty supper so the family could eat early. She saw that the children were washed and dressed in clean clothes, then took a few minutes to get ready herself.

As the family went out the back door, the wife would be certain she had her grocery list in her purse, and the children would clutch their allowances in their hands. The youngsters had to listen most of the way to town to their parents' warnings not to spend the nickel or dime or quarter foolishly, an admonition they usually ignored.

Neighbors sometimes shared rides with neighbors. For example, Pat and Fair Troxel, along with Fair's father, John, would stop at the Lewis house on the corner near their home and gather up any of the Lewis kids who wanted to go along for the Saturday night trip to Farragut.

The first stop in town was often the produce house where the farmers left their cream and eggs. While the families went on about their business, the produce workers weighed the cream and tested a sample of it to determine butterfat content, factors upon which the price of the cream was figured. They "candled" the eggs by holding each one up to a light. The light glowed through the good eggs, while spoiled eggs were dull and murky or spotted when the light was behind them. After the families had finished their other errands, they returned to the produce house and received payment for the cream and eggs.

For an hour or so each Saturday evening, the high school band members of many small towns set up their chairs and music stands near the town square, the courthouse, or the stores, and entertained everyone with a wonderful mix of marches and big band melodies. Their musicianship was often marked with more enthusiasm than accuracy. Some of the townspeople drove to the bandstand early on Saturday afternoon to park their cars on the street and then walk home. In the evening, they would walk back and sit in their cars to listen to the band and watch the crowd walking by—usually the young people or farm families who had come too late in the day to find a parking place close enough so they could sit and view the passing scene.

Larger towns like Sidney, Shenandoah, and Hamburg had indoor theaters that showed movies weeknights and also on Saturday and Sunday nights. Tickets cost fifteen cents or a quarter. Farragut tried to develop a theater in the Masonic building and sporadically had a Saturday night show, but during the time we lived in the area our favorites were those films shown outdoors by local businesspeople. To attract families to shop in their town, they erected a screen in the empty lot between the post office and the telephone building. They fashioned seats by laying boards on cement blocks and provided free movies for the entertainment of the summer Saturday night crowds. Sometimes people popped corn at home, sacked it, and brought the sacks to the makeshift theater in wire milk bottle carriers, then sold the popcorn to moviegoers for five cents a bag.

After the movie, the kids went off to find their friends and to chase one another up and down the sidewalk. The teenagers strolled along more slowly so the girls could watch to see if the boys were watching them and the boys could look to see if the girls were glancing in their direction.

As the young people in Farragut paraded up and down the street, they usually stopped in the drugstore at least once to see if any other young people were sitting on the stools along the counter and to find out if John Shepherd, son of the owner, was home from college. Saturday night sales always improved when John was home.

John created a soda fountain special he named the "Tight Wad." He began by putting a scoop of vanilla ice cream into a small Coke glass,

Herrimans' ad, April 7, 1949. Farragut Forum.

then topped it with a dollop of chocolate syrup and sprinkled chopped peanuts over the top—all for only ten cents! If the Tight Wad was too high-priced for a customer, John served up an ice cream cone for a nickel.

Meanwhile, the women went to Delbert Roberts's and Charlie Herriman's grocery stores with their lists and with the help of a clerk found the items they needed, plus a few pieces of penny candy for the children.

The men passed the time at the barbershop, where they got shaves and haircuts and had their shoes shined. A few bathed in a room at the back provided with a tub or shower. The barber and the customers always shared the latest news and jokes. As one of our neighbors told us, "I don't go to the barbershop just to get a haircut but to sit and talk about the weather, politics, and whose brother is dating whose sister." While beauty shops were well established and used by the rural women for permanents and haircuts and the dispensing of news, as far as I know, none ever provided bathing facilities.

Saturday nights were sometimes so busy that the barbers, the produce house workers, and the local café help would not close their doors until after midnight. Families with children, however, tried to get home a little earlier. With their shopping done and the groceries and empty cream cans and egg crates loaded into the car, parents found their kids and started the drive back to the farm. Sometimes the children got to the car first and curled up on the seats to nap until their parents finished their Saturday night errands, or the youngsters would check in the stores and barbershops and café to find their parents. They did not go into the taverns where some of the fathers were enjoying late beers; those establishments were off-limits to children and young ladies.

The locally owned and run small town cafés were extremely popular gathering places during those Saturday night sojourns. The one in Farragut that we knew best was owned by our long-time neighbor and friend, Emily Lewis-Bengtson. When Emmy (no one I know ever called her Emily) first opened the café, she dusted off her teapot collection, set the pots on a high shelf around the dining room, and christened the place the "Anchor Inn" in honor of the town's Civil War naval hero

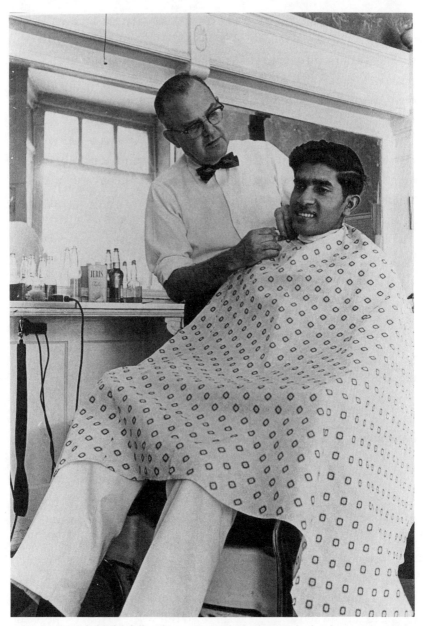

For years Herschel Whitehill and Bert Kimsey had adjoining barbershops in Farragut. In the early days, the men charged thirty-five cents for haircuts. During the depression the cost fell to twenty-five cents; a shave cost fifteen cents and a bath a quarter. By the time we moved to the farm, the price had gone up to a whopping fifty cents for each of these services. Herschel is pictured cutting the hair of W. M. Senaratne Banda, an exchange student from India. Herschel Whitehill photo.

namesake, Rear Admiral David G. Farragut. Then Emmy got out the recipes from her grandmothers Simmerman and Utterback and her mother, Mabel Lewis, and headed for the kitchen. Customers came from far and near, not just on Saturday nights but also on the other days of the week for morning coffee, breakfasts, and hearty noon dinners.

Emmy gave me many of her fine recipes while we were neighbors and during the time she owned and ran the Anchor Inn. I prepared them for my own family and shared many of them with the readers of my "Up a Country Lane" columns.

Emmy's Fried Chicken

Cut chicken into pieces and soak for a few minutes in warm water to keep the cold meat from chilling the hot shortening. This helps speed the cooking time. Combine 1 cup flour and salt and pepper to taste in a plastic or paper bag. Drain the chicken pieces and drop each in turn in the bag and shake in the flour mixture. Drop into hot canola and soybean oil mixture (half of each) until chicken is nicely brown and done inside. Emmy used lard when she first cooked on the farm but changed to the healthier shortenings when they became available.

Chicken and Biscuits

1 chicken	*4 tablespoons cornstarch*
1 large onion, chopped (at least 1 cup)	*4 tablespoons cold water*
	salt and pepper to taste
2 cups finely chopped celery	*biscuits*

Stew chicken. Remove chicken and set aside to cool. Simmer onion and celery in a little of the broth and add to main amount of broth. Blend cornstarch in cold water and stir into broth. Cook, stirring, until mixture thickens. Salt and pepper to taste. Cut chicken from bones, discard bones, and add meat to gravy. Place in a flat 9-by-13-inch baking pan and place biscuits over the top. Bake in a 400-degree oven until biscuits are brown on top. Emmy liked to use a stewing hen and then add another chicken breast and a couple of thighs so her chicken pies were full of tasty meat. Makes 6 to 8 servings.

Grocery Bars

4 eggs

2 tablespoons cold water

2 cups brown sugar, packed

2 cups sifted flour

1 teaspoon baking powder

1/2 teaspoon salt

1 teaspoon cinnamon

1 cup cut up orange candy slices

1/2 cup nuts

Combine eggs and cold water and beat well. Add brown sugar and beat until light and fluffy. Mix dry ingredients together and combine with orange slices and nuts. Stir into batter. Pour into greased 9-by-13-inch pan. Bake at 325 degrees for 25 to 30 minutes or until golden brown on top and tests done when a toothpick is inserted into the center. This is a chewy brownie, however, don't overbake. Sprinkle top with a light dusting of powdered sugar and cut while warm. A special recipe from Delbert Roberts's years as one of Farragut's grocers. Makes 12 to 15 servings.

Barbershop Gooseberry Pie

1 double-crust pie shell

3 or 4 cups of gooseberries

1 cup crushed pineapple, undrained

dash of salt

1 1/2 cups sugar

3 tablespoons cornstarch

1 tablespoon butter

Prepare 1 double-crust pie shell and line 9-inch pie pan with crust. Combine drained gooseberries (or fresh) with pineapple, salt, sugar, and cornstarch. Spoon into crust, dot with butter, and cover with top crust. Cut tiny slits in top to let steam escape. Bake at 375 degrees for 40 to 45 minutes. This was Herschel Whitehill's favorite pie.

Anchor Inn Liver and Onions

Use beef liver cut about 1/2 inch thick. Cook sliced onions separately in a little shortening in an electric skillet. Remove onions. Dip individual slices of unthawed frozen liver in a pan of very hot water, lift out, coat with flour seasoned with salt and pepper, and fry in shortening in the skillet for 1 1/2 minutes on each side—do not overcook or meat will be tough. Add 1/4 cup water and onions and cover skillet with a lid. Steam on low heat for 10 minutes or put in baking dish in a 350-degree oven. Remove liver and onions to hot platter and stir a little flour into drippings (try 2 or 3 tablespoons). When smooth, add about 1 cup of milk and stir, cooking, to make a gravy. Add more milk if needed. This gravy is delicious served with mashed potatoes. Some of the country people like to cook bacon in the skillet first and use the drippings to fry the onions and the liver for additional flavor. When Emmy gives a recipe, it may be with the same techniques her grandmother used. This recipe is a good example of one that gives the method, but you will need to decide how much liver and how many onions to use.

Ham Loaf for the Multitudes

3 pounds ground beef
3 pounds ham, ground
3 pounds lean pork, ground

12 eggs
3 cups milk
3 cups crushed graham crackers

Combine ingredients—do not add salt—make into loaves, and cover with sauce.

SAUCE

1 26-ounce can tomato soup	1 tablespoon dry mustard
1 1/2 cups brown sugar, packed	1 12-ounce can tomato sauce
1/2 cup vinegar	

Combine ingredients and coat loaves on all sides with sauce. Place each loaf in a greased bread pan or put in rows in flat baking pans. Bake at 350 degrees for 1 hour. Ham loaf was one of the favorite meats on the Anchor Inn's menu. The yield depends on how large the loaves are—probably around 8 servings in each loaf. Since this recipe is exceptionally large, it is great to use for any meal where many people need to be served. Any leftover freezes well either baked or unbaked, but you can easily cut the ingredients to make a smaller amount if desired.

Emmy's Dutch Apple Cake

2 cups flour	1 egg
3 teaspoons baking powder	2/3 cup water or fruit juice
2 tablespoons sugar	4 peeled apples
1/4 teaspoon salt	1/2 cup sugar
4 tablespoons margarine	2 teaspoons cinnamon

Mix first four ingredients and cut in margarine with a fork. Beat egg and add water or fruit juice to egg. Add liquid ingredients to dry mixture, stir, and make a stiff but moist dough. Spread in greased and floured 9-by-13-inch pan. Peel apples and cut each into 8 slices. Press slices into dough. Dot with butter. Combine sugar and cinnamon and sprinkle over apples and dough. Bake at 350 degrees for about 25 minutes. Serve with cream or hard sauce or lemon sauce. Makes about 15 pieces.

LEMON SAUCE

1 cup sugar

1/2 cup water

1 tablespoon butter

3 tablespoons lemon juice

2 teaspoons cornstarch

Combine ingredients and cook, stirring constantly, until mixture thickens, about 5 minutes. Serve over apple cake.

HARD SAUCE

1/2 cup butter

1 cup powdered sugar

1 teaspoon vanilla flavoring

Combine ingredients and beat well. Serve over apple cake.

Peanut Butter Pie

1 baked single-crust pie shell

1 8-ounce package cream cheese,

  softened

1/2 cup milk

1 cup powdered sugar

1 cup peanut butter

8-ounces frozen whipped topping

1 milk chocolate candy bar

Prepare 1 single-crust pie shell. Put cream cheese, milk, powdered sugar, and peanut butter in mixing bowl and beat well. Beat in frozen whipped topping. Spoon into baked regular pie crust or chocolate pie crust (purchased) and shave chocolate over top. Keep refrigerated.

Fruit Cocktail Bars

1/2 cup margarine

3 eggs, beaten

1 1/2 cups sugar

1 16-ounce can fruit cocktail,
    undrained

1 1/2 teaspoons baking soda

2 1/2 cups flour

1/2 teaspoon salt

1 teaspoon vanilla flavoring

1 cup flaked coconut

1 cup chopped nuts

Beat margarine, eggs, and sugar together until light and fluffy. Stir in fruit cocktail, juice and all. Blend dry ingredients together and stir in. Add flavoring, coconut, and nuts. Spoon into a 10-by-15-by-1-inch greased jelly roll pan. Bake at 350 degrees for 20 to 25 minutes. (Bake an additional 5 minutes if you use one of the air-bake pans.) Remove from oven and top with glaze. For an interesting variation use a 20-ounce can crushed pineapple, juice and all, in place of the fruit cocktail. Makes about 20 bars.

GLAZE

1 cup sugar

1/2 cup margarine

1/4 cup evaporated milk

1/2 teaspoon vanilla flavoring

Combine ingredients and boil 2 minutes, stirring occasionally. Remove from heat, cool slightly, then beat until it thickens as much as you desire. Drizzle over cake. This is a fine glaze for doughnuts, cakes, or sweet rolls.

19. Sunday Fun

Sundays were glorious family days for us during the years we lived on the farm. The end of the week was a time for fun together before the next week's labor began. It was a time to put aside routine and eliminate any work that was not essential to the well-being of the children and the livestock.

Only once did Robert do field work on Sunday. Rain threatened, and he felt he should bring out the tractor and till the corn crop before the storm. But he felt so troubled about not attending church and enjoying his family that he never again spent a Sunday in the fields. He insisted that his crops fared just as well when he worked six days a week rather than seven, and he knew he felt better physically and mentally.

Driving to the home of friends or relatives for a visit and a meal was a part of the Sunday activities for many of the families in our neighborhood. We saw our relatives frequently, so Robert and I decided to put a priority on making most Sunday afternoons a time to spend with our children. If the weather was warm, we would hurry home after church, change our clothes, pack a picnic lunch, and go to the woods. The bluffs rising above the Missouri River bottom were not far from Cottonwood Farm, and our Sundays often found us at Waubonsie State Park.

After we ate our lunch, the children would tumble in the soft grass and then encourage us to hike along the paths through the ravines and

One of Dulcie Jean's favorite spots was this spring in Waubonsie State Park where she could play in the water and get a cold fresh drink.

up to the top of the bluffs. Sometimes we saw other Sunday hikers, but more often our only companions were songbirds, hawks, wild turkeys, and an occasional eagle. We saw rabbits and squirrels, but the deer, coyotes, and foxes kept their distance, alerted by our noisy shouts and laughter.

Robert taught the children the names of the trees and explained that the tall yucca plants thriving on the sunny western slopes of the bluffs usually grow only in deserts. He showed us tumble bugs pushing tiny balls of dung filled with their eggs and scarab beetles with jewel-like,

Craig, Bob, Jeff, and I enjoy a quiet moment in the woods watching for hawks.

iridescent green shells. When we found the footprints of animals or their small skeletons, he helped us imagine what might have happened there.

In the spring we gathered morel mushrooms. In the summer we found empty cocoons and cicada shells. Come autumn, we collected acorns and black walnuts, and after the first frost we picked wild papaws that tasted like very sweet, ripe bananas.

The arrival of winter spelled the end of the year's woodland picnics, but our Sunday fun didn't stop just because of the cold. Snowfall made the slope south of our farmhouse perfect for children coasting on sleds, and the ice of Mill Creek was fine for sliding. Robert would pile little Dulcie Jean and Bob into the scoop of his big grain shovel and pull them over the ice. They screamed with delight and begged him to push them again and again until at last they were cold and tired enough to hurry back to the house for hot cocoa and toast.

Sunday evenings on the farm were quiet, a last calm before the busy rush of the week to come. Television began arriving in Iowa homes in the early 1950s, but we chose not to get one. Even after we could afford a television, we decided to put off buying one so that we would have more family time together.

Dulcie Jean brings Bob up the snowy hill south of the Cottonwood Farm.

We often began our Sunday evenings by popping enough corn to fill a dishpan. I frequently made syrup to pour over the corn so we could shape it into popcorn balls, or I made a pan of fudge or taffy, letting the children help with the stirring, beating, and pulling that was part of making those sweets.

As dusk turned into night, we played caroms, Chinese checkers, Candyland, Old Maid, Authors, and dominoes. We listened to the latest radio installments of the Lone Ranger, Fibber Magee and Molly, and the Jack Benny show. The children eventually grew drowsy and pulled on their pajamas for bed. After they were asleep, Robert and I had a few minutes left to get out the newspaper and find out what was happening in the world beyond the quiet, peaceful life of a Sunday on our farm.

Made-from-Scratch Fudge

3 cups sugar
1/4 teaspoon salt
3 tablespoons cocoa
1 cup milk

3 tablespoons white corn syrup
3 tablespoons butter
1 teaspoon vanilla flavoring
1 cup chopped nuts

In a heavy saucepan combine sugar, salt, cocoa, milk, and corn syrup. Cook, stirring, until sugar is dissolved (an important step) and mixture is smooth. Continue cooking over moderate heat, stirring as little as possible, until soft ball is formed (235 degrees on a candy thermometer). Remove from fire, add butter but do not stir. Cool to lukewarm (when the bottom of the pan is barely warm). Add flavoring. Beat with beaters or wooden spoon until mixture loses its gloss and becomes thick and creamy. Turn out into a 9-by-12-inch buttered pan. Cut into pieces. Black walnuts are wonderful in this candy. Makes about 12 pieces.

Peanut Butter Fudge

2 cups sugar
2/3 cup milk
1 cup marshmallow creme

1 cup peanut butter
1 teaspoon vanilla flavoring

Combine sugar and milk and cook until mixture forms a soft ball (235 degrees on a candy thermometer). Remove from heat and immediately stir in remaining ingredients. When well blended, pour into a 9-by-13-inch buttered pan. When cool, cut into squares. Pieces can be rolled into balls or logs if you do so while still warm and before candy is completely set. Makes 16 pieces.

Pineapple Penuche

1/2 cup brown sugar, packed

1 cup white sugar

2 tablespoons white corn syrup

1/4 cup half-and-half

1/2 cup crushed pineapple, drained

1/2 cup nuts

Combine all ingredients except for nuts and stir just to dissolve sugars. Continue boiling on moderate heat without stirring until soft ball stage (235 degrees on a candy thermometer). Add nuts, cool to lukewarm, and beat until creamy. Turn out into an 8-by-8-inch buttered pan and let cool. Makes about 12 pieces.

Peanut Brittle

3 cups sugar

1 1/2 cups white corn syrup

pinch of salt

1 1/3 cups water

3 cups raw peanuts

2 tablespoons butter

1 1/2 teaspoons baking soda

1 tablespoon water

1 teaspoon vanilla flavoring

Combine sugar, corn syrup, pinch of salt, and 1 1/3 cups water in a heavy kettle and boil until soft ball stage (235 degrees on a candy thermometer). Add raw peanuts and butter. When peanuts and syrup turn a golden brown (and pop open), remove from fire. Have the baking soda dissolved in the 1 tablespoon water and stir into hot syrup; mix carefully because the mixture will foam up. Add the flavoring. Pour out on buttered plates and let cool. Break into chunks.

Divinity

1/2 cup water

1/2 cup white syrup

2 cups sugar

2 egg whites

1/2 teaspoon vanilla flavoring

Combine water, corn syrup, and sugar. Cook, stirring to dissolve sugar. Continue boiling over moderate heat without stirring until brittle when a little is dropped in cold water (280 degrees on a candy thermometer). Beat egg whites until stiff, then continue beating while drizzling in the hot syrup. Add flavoring. When mixture holds its shape, drop onto waxed paper in little mounds. This delicate candy can be varied with different flavorings.

Taffy

3 cups sugar   3/4 cup water
3 tablespoons vinegar   1/4 teaspoon cream of tartar

Cook until brittle when tried in cold water (280 degrees on a candy thermometer). Pour on buttered plate. As soon as cool enough to handle, butter your hands and pull candy until it is white and smooth. Roll into rope shape and cut into small pieces.

Fondant

2 cups sugar   flavoring
1/8 teaspoon cream of tartar   food coloring
1/2 cup water

Combine ingredients in saucepan and stir until sugar is dissolved. Cover pan and boil 5 minutes, allowing steam to dissolve sugar on sides of pan. Uncover and continue boiling without stirring to soft ball stage (235 degrees on a candy thermometer). Wipe crystals from side of pan with damp cloth. Cool to room temperature and then beat until stiff enough to knead; knead until smooth. Add flavoring and coloring of your choice. Place in a bowl and cover with waxed paper. Chill for several hours or overnight before using. Shape into mints, stuff into dates, roll in nuts, etc. Makes about 3 dozen, depending on size.

Easy Mint Patties

1 8-ounce package cream cheese
2 pounds powdered sugar
flavoring and food coloring

Soften cream cheese to room temperature. Work in as much powdered sugar as needed to knead easily. Knead in flavoring and food coloring as desired. Shape into round flat patties, roll in granulated sugar, and make a criss-cross pattern on top with a fork or press into molds to make fancy shapes. Refrigerate or freeze until time to serve. Makes about 3 dozen.

Sparkling Gumdrops

4 envelopes unflavored gelatin
1 cup cold water
4 cups sugar

1 1/2 cups boiling water
food coloring
flavorings

Combine gelatin with cold water and soak for 10 minutes. Dissolve the 4 cups sugar in the boiling water and stir in the softened gelatin. Bring to a boil and simmer for 15 minutes. Remove from fire. Divide into bread pans or any flat pans. Color each with food coloring and flavorings of your choice—yellow with lemon, red with cherry or strawberry, green with mint. White is nice with almond. Let stand 24 hours—do not refrigerate. Dip bottom of pan in warm water to loosen candy and turn out on granulated sugar. Dip a sharp knife into hot water and cut into squares, rolling each piece well in the sugar. Place on trays covered with waxed paper—be sure the pieces do not touch one another. Cover with a tea towel and store three to four weeks to firm. These improve with age. Wonderful holiday candy.

Chocolate-Covered Cherries

1/2 cup butter or margarine
2 pounds powdered sugar

1 14-ounce can sweetened
   condensed milk
1 teaspoon vanilla flavoring

Combine ingredients and stir until well blended and smooth. Add a little more powdered sugar if mixture seems too soft. Pinch off pieces of this fondant and wrap around a maraschino cherry that has been drained well on a paper towel. Repeat with remaining fondant. Smallest cherries are best. Put on waxed paper and chill overnight. Makes about 75.

CHOCOLATE COATING

1/4 pound sweet chocolate bar
1 12-ounce package semi-sweet
  chocolate chips
1/2 cake paraffin, diced

Combine in top of double boiler over hot but *not boiling* water. Melt, stirring occasionally. When melted, turn heat very low but keep chocolate warm while you dip in the candy balls. Lift coated balls with a fork and let excess chocolate drip back into pan. Cool balls on waxed paper. When firm, wrap separately or put in little crinkle cups. These freeze well and will keep for several weeks in a cool place.

Oven Caramel Corn

8 cups popped corn

2 cups brown sugar, packed

1 cup butter or margarine

1/2 cup white corn syrup

1/2 teaspoon salt

1/2 teaspoon baking soda

peanuts (optional)

Combine brown sugar, butter or margarine, corn syrup, and salt. Boil for 5 minutes. Stir in baking soda. Pour over popped corn and peanuts and put in a large pan (or pans) and place in a 250-degree oven for 1 hour. Stir several times.

Crystallized Popcorn

8 cups popped corn

1 cup sugar

1/2 cup white corn syrup

1/3 cup water

1 tablespoon vinegar

1 tablespoon butter or margarine

1 teaspoon vanilla flavoring

1/4 teaspoon baking soda

Pop corn and remove any hard unpopped kernels. Combine sugar, corn syrup, water, vinegar, and butter or margarine in saucepan and cook until hard ball forms in cold water (280 degrees on a candy thermometer). Add flavoring and baking soda. This may foam up, so be cautious. Pour syrup over corn and put in a cool place. When cool, break apart. This can also be made into popcorn balls if pressed together while syrup is still warm.

20. Storms

~~~~~~~~~~~~~~~~~~~~~~~

During the years we lived on the farm, I became much too familiar with the phrase, "we weathered the storm." Like all farm families we experienced too much or too little of almost everything—rain, heat, cold, snow, tornadoes, blizzards. Ill-timed rains spoiled a hay crop. Drought robbed us of a corn harvest. High winds stripped the heads from ripening grain. The cost of purchasing seeds, tractor fuel, and parts for farm machinery, and the effort of planting, cultivating, and harvesting, were as great when crops were poor as when they were profitable. We had no choice but to weather the difficulties that came our way.

Most of the information about stormy conditions came to the people of Mill Creek Valley from the broadcasts beamed out by radio stations KFNF and KMA, located in nearby Shenandoah. When the weather-forecasters at the stations predicted the coming of a blizzard, their "livestock warnings" sent the farmers out into the wind to herd cattle and horses to shelter and to look after the hogs, sheep, and chickens. Like the other farm wives in the area, I checked the windows of the house to be sure they were shut tight, pulled the curtains together to keep out drafts, and prepared a warm area near the living room stove where the children could play during the blizzard. Then I went into

A winter blizzard drifted the roads until they were all but impassable. Bob Troxel photo.

the kitchen and put ground beef, canned tomatoes, and kidney beans in a kettle on the cooking stove to make a hearty meal of chili.

"What did farmers do before the days of radio?" I asked Robert as he came shivering into the house one afternoon after preparing the livestock for a storm.

"They read the *Old Farmer's Almanac*," Robert answered. "The *Almanac* hung on a nail by the kitchen door and was the most read book in the house." The *Almanac* did give all kinds of weather lore handed down from generation to generation, some of it in rhyme:

When animals huddle in the open,
It's for rain you'd best be hopin'.

Rain before seven,
Shine before eleven.

When crickets chirp loud and long,
Rain will soon come along.

Southwest Iowa is in an area known as "Tornado Alley." Max Dougan photo.

"I once overheard a farmer say that a winter would be severe because the hog he had just butchered had a thick skin," Robert continued. "Some people say that when the rings of onions are thick the winter will be hard, or that narrow bands on woolly caterpillars mean mild temperatures. I like to cut open a persimmon seed. If the white part inside is shaped like a little spoon, the winter will be warm, while a shape like a knife means a cold season ahead."

In the spring and summer, the radio stations sometimes warned us when conditions were ripe for tornadoes. There wasn't much we could do to protect the livestock, but we could seek shelter in the root cellar behind the house. Some people even called these spaces below ground level "cyclone cellars." They were the safest place on a farm to weather a tornado. I kept some emergency food there, a jar of water, a flashlight, and a portable radio.

One hot spring afternoon, we could tell from the tension in the heavy, humid air that a tornado was coming. Dark clouds, some tinged with green, swirled across the sky. Hail began to fall, stripping leaves from the crops and pounding the roofs of the farm buildings. Lightning struck a cottonwood tree near the house, splintering the branches and

When a farmstead was destroyed by a tornado, the neighbors came to help the family in any way possible. Edward May, Sr., photo.

igniting a fire high in the crown of the tree. In the distance, we could hear a roar as though a train were rumbling through the clouds.

I was ready to head for the cellar, but Robert wanted to go out into the field so he could see the broad sweep of the storm. Before we could argue about what to do, the winds began to abate and the dark clouds disappeared as quickly as they had arrived. A few minutes later, the radio announcer told us a tornado had touched down a few miles south of our farm.

The storms that farm families endured were caused not only by the weather. Illness and accidents were also part of rural life. Animals could get sick and die. A sow might lay on her piglets and suffocate them. A child could step on a rusty nail. A farmer could be injured by farm machinery.

As parents we were concerned about the health of our children. The increased use of vaccinations and antibiotics had lessened the dangers of ear infections, scarlet fever, whooping cough, smallpox, pneumonia, and other afflictions of earlier generations, but the late 1940s and early 1950s were darkened by a dreadful epidemic of polio. No one knew how it was transmitted, though children and young people were its primary targets. Churches and community clubs purchased iron lungs for hospitals where polio patients whose lungs were paralyzed could receive treatment.

While our small valley often seemed insulated from the events beyond Iowa, newspapers and radio reports kept us informed of the
world. By 1950, the Korean War was under way, and we were very
concerned about its outcome. Private First Class Dwight McMahon, a
twenty-one-year-old farm boy from Farragut, was killed on Heartbreak
Ridge in the fall of 1951. The return of his body and the memorial service brought the reality of the violence of war right into our community.

Death did not always come from far away. Our young farmer neighbor Bill Allely had died following heart surgery. Pat Troxel, our good
friend who lived up the road, was killed when his tractor rolled into a
ditch and crushed him. Jacob Schnoor, who had been such a fixture in
the area, was stricken with cancer and died.

For us, the most shattering death of all came the day after Jake
passed away. Our five-year-old daughter, Dulcie Jean, began suffering
convulsions. We rushed her to the hospital in Shenandoah, but a few
hours later she was dead. An autopsy identified the cause of death as a
virus in the heart muscles, though we never learned the origin of the
infection or why it struck so suddenly and disastrously.

The neighborhood gathered to say good-bye to Jacob Schnoor one
day and to Dulcie Jean the next. Her funeral was held at Madison Methodist Church where her body lay in state in the small entryway, the
same place where loved ones of many past generations had lain. Our
neighbors supported us with words of sympathy, the quiet touch of
hands, and heartfelt hugs.

Bringing food to a family sorrowing over a death has long been a
sign of caring for the living and respecting the dead. The women from
the Farragut and Madison churches served our relatives a dinner at the
church before the funeral. Following Dulcie Jean's burial in the Sidney
cemetery, the Friendly Fairview Club members provided a lunch for
the family at the home of Robert's parents.

For several weeks friends continued to bring tempting dishes and
encouraged us to eat and keep up our strength. We learned during
those long, painful days that the quiet offer of food provided sustenance for our bodies and comfort for our aching hearts, as our family
weathered the terrible storm of our daughter's death.

Stormy-weather foods like hot chili were prepared by farm wives when a blizzard was threatening. Mothers made "comfort dishes" for sick members of a family in the hopes the food would make the patients feel better—things like creamed dried beef on mashed potatoes or hot milk toast topped with a delicately poached egg. And many a friend prepared a special cake, a favorite salad, or her best casserole to take to a neighbor or to a funeral dinner served at the church to a family during the time of loss, some of the finest comfort foods of all.

Hot Milk Toast

1 slice toast, buttered
salt to taste
1/2 cup hot milk

Butter toast generously. Place in a wide soup bowl, salt lightly, and cut into bite-sized pieces. Pour hot milk over toast. A poached egg can be slipped on top of the toast just before pouring on the milk to add nutrition to this simple dish. It is wonderful food for someone who is ailing, recovering, feeling puny, or just not hungry for a big meal.

Stormy Weather Chili

2 medium onions, diced
1 cup diced celery
2 tablespoons cooking oil
1 1/2 pounds ground beef
4 cups canned tomatoes
1 15 1/2-ounce can chili beans

1 to 2 15-ounce cans red kidney
  beans
salt and pepper to taste
1 tablespoon sugar
1 bay leaf
2 to 3 teaspoons chili powder

Sauté onions and celery in cooking oil in large kettle or pressure pan. When golden, stir in ground beef and brown until red is gone. Stir in remaining ingredients and simmer, covered, for 1 hour. A pressure pan will lower the cooking time. Cook for about 20 minutes at 10 pounds pressure. Put pan under cold running water until pressure is down before trying to open the lid. Remove bay leaf before serving.

Cheese Rarebit

2 tablespoons butter or margarine
2 tablespoons flour
1 cup milk
3 to 4 cups American or cheddar
    cheese

1/2 teaspoon dry mustard
1/2 teaspoon Worcestershire sauce
salt and pepper to taste

Melt butter or margarine and stir in flour. When well blended, add remaining ingredients and cook over low heat, stirring, until cheese is melted and mixture is thick. Serve over toast. A little pimiento sprinkled on top adds a nice bit of color. Ham, bacon, sliced tomatoes, or pineapple can be served on the side. Serves 6 to 8.

Creamed Dried Beef on Toast

1/4 pound dried beef
3 tablespoons butter or margarine

3 tablespoons flour
2 cups milk

Shred dried beef into a skillet with the butter or margarine. Frizzle the meat over medium heat until it is heated through. Stir in the flour and keep stirring to blend and bubble. Gradually add milk. Continue cooking and stirring until mixture thickens. Serve over hot toast or mounds of mashed potatoes. Most dried beef is well seasoned, so more seasonings are not necessary. The best was home cured and dried. You can still find some in small town shops like Johnson's Locker in Essex, Iowa, where butchers still cure, dry, and slice their own. Makes about 4 servings.

Fried Potatoes

6 large cooked potatoes
1 onion, sliced

3 tablespoons shortening
salt and pepper to taste

Peel potatoes if desired or leave skins on, slice in 1/4-inch-thick slices, add sliced onion, and fry in hot shortening over medium high heat. Turn several times to brown. For hash browns, grate the potatoes and onion and combine, fry until crusty on both sides. Fresh potatoes can be used for either fried potatoes or hash browns. Simply slice or grate fresh potatoes into a skillet with hot shortening. Add onion and about 1/4 cup water. Cover and cook over moderate heat until tender, stirring once or twice. Add a little more water if needed. Remove cover and brown. Serves 6 to 8.

Breaded or Spaghetti Tomatoes

2 to 3 cups peeled and chopped ripe
    tomatoes (or 1 1-pound can
    tomatoes, undrained)
1 cup bread cubes or cooked
    spaghetti
1/2 teaspoon baking soda

2 tablespoons brown sugar, packed
1/2 cup milk or half-and-half
3 tablespoons flour
2 tablespoons butter
salt to taste

Put tomatoes in saucepan and heat to bubbly. Stir in bread cubes or cooked spaghetti. Add baking soda and brown sugar, stirring to blend. (Careful, the mixture foams up, but this eliminates the acid so the milk or cream will not curdle.) Beat milk or half-and-half and flour together until smooth and add to tomato mixture. Continue cooking, stirring, until mixture thickens slightly. Add butter and salt. Serve as a main dish, as a vegetable, or as a meat accompaniment. Serves 4 to 6.

Cornmeal Mush

4 cups water
1/2 teaspoon salt
1 cup white or yellow cornmeal

Bring water to boil. Add salt. Blend cornmeal with a little water so it will not form lumps and add to hot water, beating constantly. Cook over low to moderate heat for 15 minutes, stirring occasionally. The boiled mush can be served in a bowl with cream and sugar like a cereal, with butter, or with a poached egg and butter. Cornmeal mush can be cooked in a pressure pan by starting out as directed. When mixture is boiling, stir well and put on lid with pressure gauge. Bring to 10 pounds pressure for 5 minutes. Remove from fire and let pressure return to normal slowly. Mush can cook in microwave by combining 3 1/4 cups water in a 2-quart glass measuring cup. Beat in 1 cup cornmeal and microwave on high for 6 minutes, stirring several times, then microwave on high for another 6 minutes. For fried mush, pour hot boiled mush into a greased loaf pan and chill. Slice thick or thin as desired. Coat with flour and fry on a greased griddle. This is wonderful with cooked bacon and eggs. Some people like it with syrup and butter. Serves 6 to 8.

Crustless Quiche

1 1/2 cups milk or half-and-half　　*1 tablespoon flour*
4 eggs　　*1 1/2 teaspoons cornstarch*
1/2 teaspoon salt　　*1/4 cup sugar*
1 8-ounce package cream cheese

Combine ingredients. Whip in blender or with electric mixer. Put into 9-inch round baking pan. Sprinkle with nutmeg and bake at 375 degrees for about 20 minutes or until mixture is firm. Serves 4 to 5.

Hurry-up Chicken à la King

1 10 3/4-ounce can cream of celery
soup, undiluted
1 cup cut up cooked chicken (or
turkey)
1 4-ounce can mushrooms, stems
and pieces, drained

1 tablespoon chopped pimientos,
drained
1 teaspoon parsley flakes
salt and pepper to taste

Heat soup. Stir in remaining ingredients. Heat until bubbly and serve over toast, chinese noodles, or hot cooked rice. Serves 4.

Mabel Lewis's Comfort Jell-O

1 8-ounce can crushed pineapple,
drained
1 3-ounce package of red gelatin

2 cups white grapes
whipped cream or whipped topping

Drain pineapple. Put juice in cup and add water to make 1 cup. Heat to boiling. Dissolve gelatin in hot pineapple juice–water mixture and cool slightly. Add grapes and pineapple. Chill until firm. Serve with whipped cream or whipped topping. This was truly a comfort salad, for Mabel always took this to a family at the time of serious problems. Serves 6 to 8.

Ham Squares

1 pound cured ham, ground
1 pound lean beef, ground
1 pound lean pork, ground
1 cup crushed corn flakes

pepper to taste
2 eggs, beaten
1 cup milk

Combine ingredients. Pat into a 9-by-13-inch pan. Bake at 350 degrees for 1 hour. Add Glaze the last half hour. Cut into squares to serve.

Freezes well. This was served as the main dish at many a church function, including funeral dinners. Makes 12 to 15 servings.

GLAZE

2 tablespoons vinegar
1 teaspoon dry mustard
1/2 cup brown sugar, packed

Stir ingredients to blend. Baste as needed over loaf the last half hour of baking.

21. Auctions, a Way to Say Good-bye

M ost farmers and their families stoically accepted the challenges and uncertainties of their life-style and tried to make the best of whatever hardships came their way. But if drought or too much rain caused crops to fail, or if animals fell ill and had to be destroyed, or if livestock prices went too low, financial burdens could overwhelm a family. A farm family might decide to leave, or the landlord could ask them to vacate, or a banker might refuse to continue a loan and foreclose on the mortgage. Sometimes the move was caused by the saddest reason of all, serious illness or the death of the head of the family. Any of these circumstances could force a farm family to find a new home.

Of course, some moves were happy. Hired hands or renters might accept better positions on other farms, moving their families into more modern houses on larger acreages with more fertile soil. They might leave the farm altogether and find positions in town to improve their financial situation. An owner sometimes bought more land and moved to the better house, or purchased a different farm, sold the old and moved to the new. For whatever reason, this ritualistic, shuffling dance was usually played out across the heartland in the spring.

Moving day was traditionally March 1 so workers could get settled in a new location before the start of spring ground preparation and planting. It was not easy to leave friends and neighbors and familiar places, and the timing was especially hard for the older children if they left their familiar schools and classmates behind. But moving could also be an adventure, and it was a wise father and mother who encouraged the attitude of enjoyment in their children as they explored a new location, experienced a new school, and found new friends.

Weather at the beginning of March could be capricious, for March is still leftover winter in the Midwest—warm and pleasant one day, cold and windy the next. When rains fell at moving time the barnyards and the lanes became muddy and difficult to navigate. If the temperature dropped and the rain turned to ice and snow, the roads could become nearly impassible. Commercial moving companies were available in the cities and for those who had the money to bring them into the countryside, but all the rural folks I knew did their own moving with their trucks or wagons and sometimes the help of a neighbor or two.

The event that more than any other signaled change for rural folks was the announcement of an auction sale. A farmer would hire an auctioneer and place ads in the local newspapers and on the radio stations. A crowd would gather at the appointed time, and the husband would sell the machinery and livestock he did not want or could not move to a different property. His wife would sort all the household items she no longer needed and sell them, too. If a death had occurred, everything the family owned would often be offered for purchasers to view and buy. Whatever the cause behind an auction, it was always a kaleidoscope of color, sounds, and sights.

No one dressed up for an auction sale in a barnyard, except perhaps an antique dealer who wanted to be noticed. Most of the men wore their usual blue jeans and weathered denim jackets with red or green plaid linings. Their caps, given out by seed corn dealers, displayed brightly colored company emblems. A few men wore bib overalls and chewed on fat brown cigars. Older farm women wore print dresses and pulled on sweaters if the weather was cool. Younger wives and the girls opted for slacks and jackets, simple everyday work clothes.

Many who attended farm auctions were family friends who wanted

Closing Out Sale

Due to the death of my husband, I will sell all my livestock and equipment at the Nellie Feil farm, located 5 miles south of Farragut on a gravel road, on

WEDNESDAY, DEC. 12

—Starting Promptly at 12:30 P. M.—

22 -- Head of Cattle -- 22

One Jersey cow to freshen in January; One Roan spotted cow to freshen in January; One Holstein to freshen in January, extra good; One Brindle cow to freshen in January, extra good; One 2-yr. old Roan heifer, fresh two weeks; Three Shorthorn stock cows to freshen early Spring; Two yearling steers, approximately 850 lbs.; 5 head of yearlings; Five head of Spring calves; Shorthorn calf, 3 weeks old.
Twenty Head Spring Pigs, Wt. 175 lbs., Vaccinated.

—COMPLETE LINE OF—
Ford Machinery

1949 Ford tractor, starter lights, extra good tires, belt pulley; 2-row cultivator; 2-row lister; 7 ft. Ford power mower; 2-bottom gang plow; 1949 single row Woods Bros. picker, picked 90 acres; Ford power jack. All this equipment bought new in 1949. Kelly Ryan all steel 36-ft. elevator, new in '48; J. D. hoist and steel jack; IHC side delivery rake; 2-row stalk cutter; 3-section IHC harrow; 10 ft. IHC disc; IHC endgate seeder; dump rake; horse mower; rubber-tired two-wheel trailer; high wheel wagon; 2 Brady wagons on rubber with Pitzenburger wide boxes, year old and like new; hay rack with steel running gear; tumble bug.

Miscellaneous

300 gal. gas barrel on stand, hose and nozzle; 2 oil-burning tank heaters; DeLaval cream separator; all kinds of farm tools, forks, shovels, etc.; Gas barrels; slat cribbing; 10x12 brooder house on skids; bottle gas brooder stove, new last year; some panel gates; some miscellaneous household goods; miscellaneous hog troughs, etc.
110 White Rock pullets. Selling to Hamburg Hatchery, laying now. A nice flock of pullets.

Hay and Grain

700 bales red clover hay. All good hay. Approximately 1300 bushels good dry corn in crib; Approximately 300 bushels oats in bin.

TERMS— CASH

LUNCH ON GROUNDS
—Riverton Community Club

MRS. MILLARD ALLELY

Ferrell Allely

Administratrix of the Estate of Millard F. Allely

McIntyre Bros. & Paul Bell,
AUCTIONEERS

Nishna Valley State Bank,
CLERK

REMEMBER THE DATE—WEDNESDAY, DECEMBER 12—12:30 p.m.

Ferrell Allely's sale bill in the Shenandoah Evening Sentinel.

People are looking over household items ready for an auction sale.

to buy a memento of someone they had known. Others were looking for bargains, often a piece of farm machinery they hoped to purchase for less than the price of new equipment. If the sellers were older people, antique shopkeepers came to glean treasured pieces of furniture, handmade quilts, or prized dishes that they could resell in their shops.

The farm family and the auctioneer's crew would have everything on display before the bidding began. Near the barn would be the tractors, plows, corn pickers, seeders, manure spreaders, barrels, pitchforks, and stacks of odds and ends that looked like junk but might include exactly the part another farmer needed to repair some broken equipment. The pens nearby held livestock and poultry noisily announcing displeasure at their confinement.

Furniture and household appliances were placed in neat rows in the yard near the house, where they were piled high with stacks of folded towels, pillow cases, sheets, and quilts. Lamps, dishes, pots, pans, and fruit jars stood on long wooden tables. Boxes on the ground held books and magazines. Here and there were family heirlooms—an orange-colored carnival glass bowl, a gleaming cut-glass pitcher, or delicately

A farm machinery auction sale. Dale Brooks photo.

etched crystal goblets. A box or two held bright costume jewelry, embroidered handkerchiefs, and colorful neck scarves. Others contained Christmas decorations, stationery, pens, and pencils. They were usually sold by the box, so everyone who came early searched carefully for a treasure or two the auctioneer might overlook and thus sell the box at a lower price than if the real value of what it held were known.

I attended every auction I could, not so much to buy as to observe. At first I found the auctioneer's rapid patter difficult to follow, but after several auctions I began to understand the bidding process. I also noticed that since people didn't want to bid against their friends, they pretended they were among strangers once the auction started. After the buying was over, neighbors were neighbors once more.

The saddest circumstances were when sickness or a death forced a family off the farm. Women like Myrtle Brooks did manage farms they owned following the deaths of their husbands, but the situation for tenant wives was different. Renting gave a family a tenuous hold on the land. If a man could no longer work, the rent could no longer be paid, and the family would be asked to move so that an able-bodied farmer could take over. All owners were reluctant to rent land to women, especially to young mothers such as Ferrell Allely.

Soon after Bill Allely's death in September of 1951, Ferrell's landlady made arrangements to lease the farm to another family. She informed Ferrell and her three children that they would have to vacate the house by March 1. Rather than spend a winter on the farm alone with her three children, Ferrell rented a house in Shenandoah and made plans to move before Christmas. In mid-December, the neighbors came to the Allely place for the second time that year. They had come in November to harvest the crops. This time they arrived for the auction sale of everything Ferrell no longer needed, including Bill's farm machinery, twenty-two head of cattle, 110 white rock chickens, and a red rooster the children considered a pet. The rooster sold for fifty dollars due to the extravagant bidding of friends who used this as one more way to help.

Shortly after the sale, the neighbors brought in their farm trucks and helped Ferrell move her remaining belongings to Shenandoah. By the time she and her children arrived at their new house, their friends had unloaded everything, arranged the furniture, and given the place the look of a home.

Ferrell and her family made new friends in town. People from Mill Creek Valley stopped by for a time to be certain the family was adjusting, and when she could, Ferrell attended the Friendly Fairview Club meetings and neighborhood activities. Then, as we knew she should, her ties with the old place and the farm people lessened.

Robert and I did not make it as farmers either. We did the best we could with what we had for seven years, but in early spring of 1955 we became players in the game of changing homes. As was true with many others after World War II, we had followed our dream to the countryside, but we found no pot of gold at the end of any of our rainbows. None of the years we lived on Cottonwood Farm was good financially. With part of the income going to the landlord for rent, 120 acres was just not enough land to provide the money we needed to take care of our growing family.

Starting in 1953, Robert had supplemented our income by working

Through the years we continued to have family gatherings with good food and fellowship around our table. Left to right: Oliver Bricker, Craig, Bob, Larry Lynn Bricker, Robert, Ruth Bricker, Jeffrey, and Grandma Corrie.

part-time for the Fremont County Agricultural Stabilization and Conservation Service in Sidney. When the A.S.C.S. county committee offered him the full-time position as county executive director in August of 1954, Robert was delighted to accept the opportunity. He would still be involved with agriculture and in direct contact with the farm families of the county, including all of our Mill Creek Valley neighbors. He would also be assured of a regular and adequate salary.

The sale we had before we moved was simple compared to many. Robert sold most of his livestock and the few pieces of machinery he did not plan to take with him to use in the big garden he wanted to plant at the new place.

The house we rented was two miles south of Sidney. The basement was spacious enough for the washer and rinse tubs and had built-in cupboards for our homegrown and home-canned food. It also had a coal-fired furnace with heating pipes that ran from the firebox to every room upstairs, which meant that the bulky oil-burning stove I had so much disliked at Cottonwood Farm did not make the move with us. Besides five large rooms, a broad front porch, and a small back porch, the house had a real bathroom—oh joy!

Our new home also had an electric water pump instead of a windmill. Near the pump stood a chicken house and a fenced lot for the sheep and heifers Robert brought with us. Just south of the house stood a small grove of trees whose leaves supplied shade and shelter where fireflies sparkled in the summer evenings. Beneath the trees flowed a spring-fed brook. Its water held tadpoles in the spring and provided great wading pools for the children in the summer. In winter, its frozen surface was as good a sliding spot as had been the ice of Mill Creek.

It was not easy to leave Cottonwood Farm and our dream of being farmers. When we had the last of our belongings loaded, we walked through the empty house and realized that a chapter in our lives had come to an end. As Robert shut and fastened the barnyard gate for the final time, I began to think of what was to come—new friends to be made, new adventures to be experienced, new challenges to be discovered. Then, gradually, Robert revved up the motor, shifted gears, and we started down the lane.

During the auction sale days on the farms, the women of a church group or a country social club would set up tables in a garage or shed and sell snack foods as a way to raise money for their projects. Many of their favorite sale recipes became mine as well.

Raised Doughnuts

1 cup mashed potatoes
2 packages yeast
1/2 cup lukewarm water
1 cup milk
1/3 cup butter or margarine

1/2 cup sugar
1/2 teaspoon salt
2 eggs, beaten
5 cups flour (about)

Put mashed potatoes in mixing bowl. Dissolve yeast in lukewarm water. Scald milk and add to mashed potatoes. Stir in butter or margarine, sugar, and salt and blend well. When lukewarm, beat in eggs and yeast mixture and enough flour to make dough that can be kneaded. Do not use any more flour than necessary. Knead several minutes on lightly floured board. Place in greased bowl and cover. Let rise until double, punch down, and let rise again. Turn out on board and knead

2 minutes, then roll or pat out 1/2 inch thick and cut with a round cutter—do not cut holes. Let rise until double. Pull hole in center with fingers, stretch to size of half dollar. Drop into hot shortening, about 370 degrees or when a bread cube sizzles when dropped in. Drop doughnuts in flat side up so they will continue rising while they cook. Glaze while warm. Set on wire rack with a plate underneath to catch drips. Makes about 3 dozen.

GLAZE

1 pound powdered sugar
3 tablespoons butter or margarine
1 tablespoon half-and-half

1/2 teaspoon vanilla flavoring
water enough to make a soft
   frosting

Combine ingredients and drizzle over hot doughnuts.

Applesauce Doughnuts

2 tablespoons butter
1 cup brown sugar, packed
2 eggs
1 teaspoon baking soda
3 teaspoons baking powder
1/3 teaspoon salt

4 cups flour
3/4 teaspoon cinnamon
1/2 teaspoon cloves
1/4 teaspoon nutmeg
1 cup applesauce

Cream together the butter and sugar, beat in the eggs. Combine dry ingredients and stir into creamed mixture alternately with applesauce. Add a little more flour if needed to bring dough to rolling consistency. Roll or pat out on lightly floured breadboard to about 1/2 inch thick and cut with a doughnut cutter. Fry in deep hot shortening, about 370 degrees or when a bread cube sizzles when dropped in. Turn doughnuts once to brown on both sides. Drain on paper towels. Sprinkle with granulated sugar while still warm. These can be made into plain cake doughnuts by using 1 cup of milk in place of the applesauce. Makes about 3 dozen.

Sloppy Joes

1 pound ground beef
3/4 cup finely chopped onion
salt and pepper to taste
1 10 3/4-ounce can chicken gumbo
    soup

2 tablespoons catsup
1 tablespoon prepared mustard
hamburger buns

Brown ground beef and onion in a small amount of shortening. Season with salt and pepper as desired. Stir in remaining ingredients and simmer about 15 minutes or until flavors are blended. Spoon onto hamburger buns. Serves 8 to 10.

Pressed Chicken Sandwiches

1 stewing chicken
3 cups water
1 onion

4 or 5 stalks celery
seasonings

Combine ingredients and stew until chicken is tender, drain and reserve broth, remove meat from bones, and chop fine with a knife. Pack chopped chicken in bread pan and cover with broth. Press down with a pint fruit jar laid sideways if desired or just let it set up to make a loaf firm enough to slice for sandwiches. Makes enough for about 25 sandwiches, depending on the size of the chicken.

Chicken Sandwich Treat

1 cup chopped cooked chicken
1/4 cup chopped English walnuts
1/4 cup chopped celery

2 tablespoons mayonnaise
2 tablespoons salad dressing

Combine ingredients. Spread on buttered bread, top with lettuce. Makes enough for about 4 sandwiches.

Carrot-Raisin-Peanut Spread

1 cup ground carrots　　　　　*3/4 cup ground peanuts*
3/4 cup ground raisins　　　　*mayonnaise*

Grind carrots, raisins, and peanuts through food grinder or in food processor. Mix in enough mayonnaise to moisten. Excellent for a sandwich spread on any kind of buttered bread. This can also be used as a salad. Makes enough for about 6 sandwiches.

Shrimp Sandwich Spread

1 1/2 ounces cream cheese　　　*salt and pepper to taste*
1/2 cup chopped cooked shrimp　*1 tablespoon mayonnaise*

Soften cream cheese to room temperature and combine with remaining ingredients, blending well. Spread on buttered bread. Makes enough for 2 or 3 sandwiches.

Stuffed Olive Spread

1 3-ounce package cream cheese　　*1/4 cup chopped nuts*
1/4 cup sliced stuffed green olives　*1/4 teaspoon paprika*
1/4 cup finely chopped celery

Soften cream cheese to room temperature and combine with remaining ingredients. Makes enough for about 4 sandwiches.

Chicken-Ham Spread

1 cup finely cut cooked chicken　　*1/2 cup sliced stuffed green olives*
1 cup finely cut cooked ham　　　*mayonnaise*

Combine ingredients with enough mayonnaise to moisten. Spread on buttered bread. Makes enough for about 6 sandwiches.

Tuna Sandwich Spread

1 6 1/8-ounce can tuna, drained

3 hard-cooked eggs

3 tablespoons finely chopped sweet
  pickles

1/4 cup finely chopped celery

1/4 teaspoon paprika

salt to taste

mayonnaise or salad dressing

Combine ingredients with enough mayonnaise or salad dressing to moisten. Spread on buttered bread. Makes enough for about 6 sandwiches.

Cheese Sandwich Filling

3/4 pound American or cheddar
  cheese

1 teaspoon prepared mustard

1/4 cup finely chopped sweet pickles

1 small jar pimientos, drained and
  chopped

mayonnaise

Grind or chop cheese in food processor. Combine with remaining ingredients and add enough mayonnaise to moisten. Spread on buttered bread. Makes enough for 8 to 10 sandwiches.

Afterword

~~~~~~~~~~~~~~~~~~~~~

During the years we lived on Cottonwood Farm, it sometimes seemed as though nothing would ever change. I would stand in the cool shadows beneath the cottonwood trees and drink in the beauty of Mill Valley, our fields, and the meandering creek. I was content in knowing that this farm, sheltering and nurturing the people I loved most, was at this moment our own. It was home.

But nothing ever stays the same. The rapid changes occurring in rural communities following World War II would only accelerate. At mid-century, a hard-working farm family could make a living on a hundred acres of land. Today, a farmer needs 600 to 1,000 acres to stay in business. As the costs of machinery, seeds, and fertilizer increased and the prices farmers received for their crops stayed low, most small land-owners and renters gave up and saw their land absorbed into larger farm operations.

It has been a long time since people crowded the streets of Farragut on a Saturday night. While the bank is still open, the hotel has become an antique shop, Roberts's grocery has been converted into a senior citizens' center, and the drugstore where John Shepherd used to make his famous Tight Wad sundaes is a tavern. The Masons and Eastern Star members continue to meet in their building, and a new fire station has been built down the street not far from where Central worked in the old telephone exchange building. Both barbershops are closed, and

239

Herriman's is now James Country Grocery. The Anchor Inn still serves home-cooked noontime meals, but Emmy has retired and only comes in now and then to bake a pie or make up a pan of her special cinnamon rolls.

The Mill Creek Valley neighborhood has changed dramatically. A few of the descendants of the original families still own and work the fields, and some of the women continue to get together for meetings of the community social clubs. But many of the homes and barns have been bulldozed and burned so that the last bits of land could be planted with crops. The Allely place is gone, as are all the buildings on Jake Schnoor's Osage Farm. The Bricker homeplace on my sister's farm has been leveled.

Our house at Cottonwood Farm is gone, too, and so is the barn and all the other buildings except a small machine shed. Even the cottonwood trees have been cut down and the brooks from the springs dammed to make way for more rows of soybeans and corn.

As farm families left the area, the Madison church finally closed. The building was demolished a few years ago, and the site where we so often gathered to worship with our neighbors now lies under a sea of corn.

So much has changed on the land, and so many people are gone. And yet it is easy for me to close my eyes and remember those days when we were young and full of dreams. I can still see picnics in the churchyard on warm summer nights and how we all pitched in to repair the building or celebrate important events in our lives. I can still feel the joy of swaying high atop a wagonload of June hay on the way from the alfalfa field to the barn and can hear the corn pickers clanking through the fields in the golden days of autumn.

I can remember the gleeful shouts of my children as their father pulled them in a scoop shovel across the ice of Mill Creek. In my mind I can be close again to that little girl in pigtails as she chases kittens down a hill and that little boy as he helps his daddy carry buckets of milk in from the barn.

Finally, I can always see the long country lane that led to Cottonwood Farm. We had driven up it at the beginning of our farming adventure full of enthusiasm and hope. And we had made our way back down the lane when we left the farm for the last time. Despite the hard work and the setbacks, our years at Cottonwood Farm had made us so much wiser, so much stronger, and, I hope, so much better for having been there. Best of all, they had filled each of us with a lifetime of wonderful memories of a time and a place and a way of life that will never come again.

Recipe Index

Bur Oak Books

"All Will Yet Be Well": The Diary of Sarah Gillespie Huftalen, 1873–1952
By Suzanne Bunkers

A Cook's Tour of Iowa
By Susan Puckett

The Folks
By Ruth Suckow

Fragile Giants: A Natural History of the Loess Hills
By Cornelia F. Mutel

An Iowa Album: A Photographic History, 1860–1920
By Mary Bennett

Iowa Birdlife
By Gladys Black

Landforms of Iowa
By Jean C. Prior

More han Ola og han Per
By Peter J. Rosendahl

Neighboring on the Air: Cooking with the KMA Radio Homemakers
By Evelyn Birkby

Nineteenth Century Home Architecture of Iowa City: A Silver Anniversary Edition
By Margaret N. Keyes

Nothing to Do but Stay: My Pioneer Mother
By Carrie Young

Old Capitol: Portrait of an Iowa Landmark
By Margaret N. Keyes

Parsnips in the Snow: Talks with Midwestern Gardeners
By Jane Anne Staw and Mary Swander

A Place of Sense: Essays in Search of the Midwest
Edited by Michael Martone

Prairie Cooks: Glorified Rice, Three-Day Buns, and Other Reminiscences
By Carrie Young with Felicia Young

Prairies, Forests, and Wetlands: The Restoration of Natural Landscape Communities in Iowa
By Janette R. Thompson

A Ruth Suckow Omnibus
By Ruth Suckow

"A Secret to Be Burried": The Diary and Life of Emily Hawley Gillespie, 1858–1888
By Judy Nolte Lensink